Tony Chachere's
Second Helping

≈ *A Lifetime Collection of the* ≈
Ole Master's Favorite Cajun & Creole Recipes

Published by Tony Chachere's Creole Foods of Opelousas, Inc.
P.O. Box 1687, Opelousas, Louisiana 70571

Customer Service 1-800-551-9066

i

First Edition

First printing, September 1995

© 1995 by Tony Chachere's Creole Foods of Opelousas, Inc.

Printed in Singapore

Dedication

———⟫⟩-0-⟨⟪———

This work is dedicated to the memory of my loving wife, Patricia Kerr Chachere, who kept me on course. She shared my enthusiasm for the preparation of a good meal and always saw to it that it was executed with the utmost attention to detail, style, and etiquette. I also dedicate the book to my five children, Donald A. Chachere, Sr., Patricia Chachere Castille, Alexander B. Chachere, Douglas J. Chachere, Sr., and Jeannine Chachere Wallace. My children and their families are the great joy of my life.

Foreword

I first met Mr. Tony years ago at a jambalaya judging at Pop's, a little place on the banks of False River. We were judging pots of jambalaya created by cooks from the New Roads area, and every one of them was convinced that his or her batch was the absolute best--no contest.

I was new to the judging game, but I realized that judging food in south Louisiana is like judging babies anywhere else in the country. You don't want to tell a mama her baby is ugly, and you don't want to tell a Cajun cook that his jambalaya (or gumbo, or etouffée, or sauce piquant, or boudin, etc.) isn't as good as someone else's. So I was glad an authority figure like Mr. Tony was on hand to lend his tall, regal presence to the proceedings. I deferred to him in the judging, confident that while the cooks may protest the opinion of a newspaper guy from Baton Rouge, nobody was going to challenge Mr. Tony's verdict.

Sure enough, when he announced the winner there was only some mild grumbling from the losers; whereas, if I had been there alone, there's a good chance the losers would have felt compelled to toss me into False River.

Pop's is no longer with us, but the friendship I struck up with Mr. Tony Chachere that night has endured.

Like everyone else who's come in contact with the extraordinary gent, I've been amazed at his vast knowledge of Cajun and Creole cooking, his multitude of friends and admirers all over this area, and his savoir faire-his knack of keeping his cool no matter what the situation.

For example, I once judged a beef cooking contest with him that was held in Opelousas in August, in a metal building. For those of you who live in this part of the country, I've said enough. If you live in cooler climes, I'm talking HOT, me!

To make it worse, the metal structure was filled with people cooking over charcoal grills, propane burners, camp stoves, etc.

I wound up judging in a T-shirt and shorts. A lady judging with us, who had the foresight to dress for the weather, stripped down to shorts and a swimsuit top. Mr. Tony showed up wearing a white suit, white shirt and tie and white shoes, and looking as neat and serene as could be imagined.

During the long judging period, as the

temperature continued to climb, Mr. Tony did not remove his coat, did not seem to notice the heat, and did not even noticeably perspire. Now THAT'S keeping your cool!

I've been fortunate enough to run into Mr. Tony at various food events all over the state, and at purely social ones, too. When mutual friend Don Williams of New Roads sets up his mobile home along that city's main drag at Mardi Gras time, you can count on Mr. Tony to be there, pressing the flesh as he greets hordes of admirers, grinning at their jokes, and handing out samples of his extraordinary spices.

His zest for living and his love of good food make him an arch-typical Cajun. More than anyone else I know, he embodies the qualities we associate with Acadiana and its people.

There are other products you always seem to find on Cajun tables--Tabasco and Community Coffee come to mind--but the round green Tony Chachere seasoning can is the one universally-used product that's identified with a person and not a company.

On my stove, and at my table, there are containers labeled "Salt" and "Pepper" and "Mr. Tony's." No one, and I've had visitors from as far away as Minnesota, has ever asked me, "What is 'Mr. Tony's?'."

Then there are his great cookbooks, from which this kid from Mississippi has learned to cook crawfish, crabs, shrimp, red snapper, gator, turtle, and all the wonderful delicacies that make south Louisiana a gourmand's paradise.

As Mr. Tony enters his ninth decade, those of us who have spent time with him and shared his good humor and amazing cooking skills can consider ourselves very lucky. For whenever anyone asks us, "What is a Cajun and what's so special about them?", we will always have the answer: "Mr. Tony Chachere."

Smiley Anders

Introduction

I love good food and I love to cook. For that matter, I love to eat. I find it very gratifying to prepare a meal, and I don't mind a compliment or two for my efforts.

Folks always ask me, "Where did you learn to cook?" and "How did you come up with the idea to make your famous seasoning?" There are no short answers to these questions. There are colorful stories which collectively answer the "where" and the "how."

I savored my mother's delicious cooking as a child. Although she never let me stir in a pot, I learned a lot by observing, peeling, chopping, and shucking.

My first real cooking experience resulted from a trip to a fishing camp back in 1930 when I was in my early twenties. Just as braggin' rights are awarded the fellow with the biggest catch, so are they awarded to the one who can cook 'em best back at the camp.

The cook on that trip was my brother-in-law's father. He served one incredibly delicious gaspergou courtbouillon. I wanted to cook like that!

Over the next two decades, I went to druggist school, then started my own wholesale drug business. I learned to mix ingredients.

When I had the production part of the business in full operation, I took to the open road, selling my products all along the Gulf Coast.

I ate in many little diners along the way. I met many folks who shared their cooking secrets with me. There were many hunting and fishing trips with customers where I got to learn from some excellent camp cooks and got to practice my cooking skills. I was slowly becoming pretty good at it!

During the early 1950s, I entered the insurance business, and also became a charter member of an all men's culinary group called Cooks Unlimited. This was a great forum for sharpening my cooking skills. Every member of this group took a turn as chef du jour at our fortnightly dinners.

One evening I observed one of my culinary brothers mixing his salt and red and black peppers together in a large bowl to season his birds for the evening meal. The idea hit me that I was accustomed to using seven favorite spices every time I cooked. That evening at home I pre-mixed my spices and stored the mixture in a large jar.

For camp trips, I would scoop out a bit of

my seasoning mix to take along instead of lugging all seven jars or shakers of my favorite spices. I used the mix on my turns as chef at Cooks Unlimited. Word spread about my "secret" mix and soon I was making many jars of the mix for family, friends, and insurance customers.

During the late 1960s, I set about collecting recipes to put together a cookbook. I knew when I retired from the insurance business that I wanted to devote my time to cooking. My desire was to share the Creole style of cooking of my roots as well as the Cajun style that was so much a part of my life.

I fulfilled my desire when my Cajun Country Cookbook was published in 1972, years before "Cajun" was a hot national phenomenon. I used my own seasoning mix in many recipes in the book. As people acquired copies of the cookbook, they wrote to me for instructions as to where they could buy the seasoning mix. I started packing jars of the seasoning for these customers. In the next editions of the cookbook, I placed order blanks for the seasoning mix. Within a couple of years, I had so many orders I decided I must really have a product that people wanted. So

in 1976, Creole Foods of Opelousas was born and we developed a green shaker can for my "Famous Creole Seasoning."

So now you know how I learned to cook and how my famous seasoning came about. I've been cooking now for over 65 years. I've learned many tricks, collected many recipes, made many friends, and shared many fine meals along the way. I never dreamed that my seasoning mix would be a staple in Louisiana kitchens. Outside Louisiana, most folks that use it still can't say my last name, but they know it comes in a green can.

My first cookbook is 23 years old now. As my 90th birthday approaches, I felt it was time for a second book. This one is a collection of all my favorite recipes as well as a storybook of some of the fun I've had along the way.

So hold out your plate and get ready to enjoy as I serve up a "second helping."

Acknowledgments

There is a collection of people whom I gratefully acknowledge for their valuable contributions to this book.

First and foremost, there are a number of people who unselfishly shared recipes with me over the years. I learned so much from them. You'll come to know many of them through stories in this book. To these special friends, my deepest gratitude.

Next, the charter members of Cooks Unlimited, most of whom are gone but not forgotten. The ten years of fortnightly suppers we shared together certainly turned this gourmand into a gourmet.

Throughout the book, particular friends appear in photos with me or lent their homes or establishments for our pictorials. Thank you to Camille Chachere, Obbie Bordelon, Jude Tauzin, Miss Yambilee 1995 Shannon Dickson, Grady Crosslin, Dwayne Brasseux, Keith Blanchard, Errol Verret, Al Berard, Jimmy Dubuisson, Vance Mamalakis, and Hugh Thistlethwaite for appearing with me in these photos. Thanks to the staff of the Academy of the Sacred Heart in Grand Coteau, Vermilionville, and Randol's Restaurant in Lafayette, the Steamboat Warehouse in Washington, and shrimpers in Delcambre for hosting us for photo shoots. Thanks also to E. J. and Jowella Ardoin of Carencro and Bill and Dorris Copeland of Butte La Rose for their hospitality and the use of their lovely homes; and to Burnell Savant who graciously loaned us props for photos as did the owners of Toby's Little Lodge, Soileau's Dinner Club, Prejean's Restaurant, and Enola Prudhomme's Cajun Cafe.

Photography throughout this cookbook, as on many of my projects, was done by the remarkable Paul Rico of New Orleans. If anyone can make me look good, he's the one! Food styling for the cover photo was accomplished by Martha Torres and her assistant Rosalind Richard. Food and floral styling on the eight sectional photographs was the work of Virginia Moseley of New Orleans. These ladies sure made my recipes look fantastic!

Lastly, I owe a huge debt of gratitude to the team who assisted me in this endeavor:

Todd Ardoin	Janice LeBlanc
Donald A. Chachere, Jr.	Pat McGlothlin
Nanette Fisher	Helen Timmerman
Diana Gradney	

Table of Contents

"I picked berries mostly
to stay out of trouble
and in my Mama's good graces."

HOME COOKING

BERRY PICKIN'

Do you remember summer afternoons of berry picking? The mere thought of it just makes me itch all over.

Most of my family enjoyed picking blackberries along the barbed wire fences throughout the countryside. I picked berries mostly to stay out of trouble and in my Mama's good graces.

It was so much fun to roam through the woods and fields, tramping through tall grasses, finding new swimming holes, making trails to return to the next day.

Since school was out in summer, it was easy to lose track of time. That's when a gallon syrup can tied to my hip would really come in handy. I knew if I toted home a can full of blackberries, it would make my Mama overlook how late I was in coming home.

I learned from Mama to pick 'em when they were nice and plump and dark purple in color. I tried to avoid the stickers on the vine, but I'd always end up with plenty scratches on my arms. Once I'd fill the syrup can with as much as I could carry, it was time to head home. I'd always manage to avoid a little snake or two on the trail toward home.

Mama knew what I'd been up to by the purple stains on my hands. She praised my efforts and put my pretty berries to soak right away. And she wouldn't punish me.

She didn't have to. About midnight, I would begin to feel the result of my day in the woods. My little body would itch like mad from the bites of the dreaded redbugs.

Some ladies used their blackberries to make tarts back then. Some made pies, some even made wine. But Mama stuck to her favorite cobbler recipe. The rest of my berries ended up as preserves to enjoy during leaner times of the year.

I can still remember the taste of that warm blackberry cobbler with a big glass of milk. Definitely helped me forget the itching for a while!

HOME COOKING
Contents

HOME COOKING
Contents

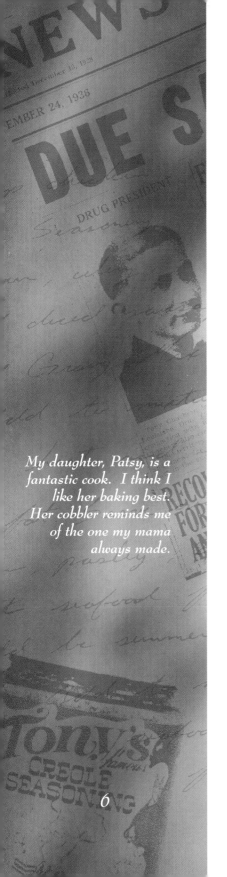

BLACKBERRY FILLING

1 cup sugar   4 cups fresh blackberries
¼ cup water

Wash berries and drain. Mix sugar and water in a large pot and bring to a boil. Add berries and cook for 20 to 30 minutes until the mixture is thick. Stir often to prevent sticking. Yields 4 cups.

PATSY'S BLACKBERRY COBBLER

Crust

1½ cups biscuit mix   2 tablespoons sugar
½ cup milk

Filling

4 cups blackberry filling   2 tablespoons sugar
¼ stick butter or margarine

In a bowl, mix together ingredients for crust. Roll out ⅔ dough for bottom crust, saving the remaining dough. Fit into 1 quart loaf pan. Add blackberry filling and dot with butter. Roll out remaining dough and place on top of berries. Bring sides of bottom crust over and seal. Sprinkle with sugar; cut 1 or 2 slits in top to let steam escape. Bake at 400° for 30 to 40 minutes or until golden brown. You may substitute any fresh fruit. Yields 6 servings.

My daughter, Patsy, is a fantastic cook. I think I like her baking best. Her cobbler reminds me of the one my mama always made.

6

BLACKBERRY JELLY

6 quarts blackberries   3 cups sugar
1 pint water

Wash berries, half of which should be red, and in a medium stock pot, cook slowly in water for 15 minutes, mashing during cooking time to extract juice. After cooking, strain through colander, mashing again to extract all of the juice.

If you did not have many red berries, add the juice of $\frac{1}{2}$ lemon to jelly stock for pectin. Strain jelly stock through cheesecloth. Return liquid to stock pot; add sugar to the cold stock; heat slightly. Stir until the sugar is dissolved, then cook rapidly until the jelly stage is reached (222° F.).

Remove from heat and allow the syrup to stop boiling. Skim and pour gently into hot sterilized jars. As soon as the jelly sets, the jars are ready to seal. Yields 8 (4 oz.) containers.

FIG PRESERVES

$\frac{1}{2}$ cup baking soda   5 pounds sugar
2 gallons water   2 lemons, thinly sliced
2 gallons figs

In a large pot, dissolve soda in water and soak figs 15 minutes. Rinse thoroughly and drain. Put figs in a large heavy saucepan with sugar and lemons. Start cooking on very low heat until sugar melts, stirring to prevent sticking. Gradually increase heat to medium and allow mixture to simmer, uncovered, for $1\frac{1}{2}$ to 2 hours, or until mixture reaches desired consistency. Pour into hot jars and seal immediately. Yields 12 pints.

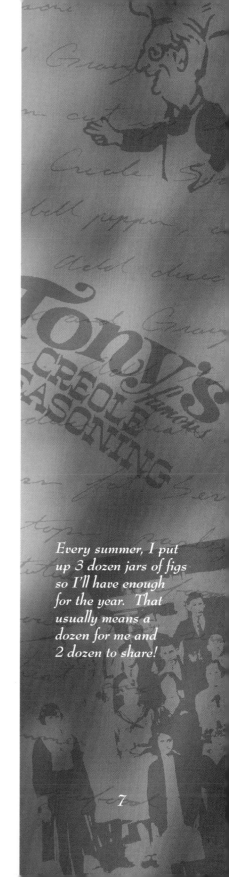

Every summer, I put up 3 dozen jars of figs so I'll have enough for the year. That usually means a dozen for me and 2 dozen to share!

7

SWEET DOUGH PIES

4 tablespoons margarine
3/4 cup sugar
1 egg
1 teaspoon vanilla extract

2 3/4 cups all-purpose flour
2 teaspoons baking powder
1/4 teaspoon salt
1/4 cup milk

In a bowl, cream margarine and sugar. Add egg and vanilla. Add flour, salt, and baking powder alternately with milk. Knead into a soft dough and chill. Roll out into eight 6 inch circles.

Filling for Tarts or Sweet Dough Pies

Fig Preserves
Bouillie (Vanilla Custard)
Orange Marmalade

Blackberry Preserves
Any Flavor Pudding

Spoon about 2 tablespoons of filling onto half of the circle of dough. Fold dough over filling, forming a half moon shape. Press edges closed with a fork. Bake in 350° oven until edges turn golden. Yields 8 pies.

PECAN PIE

3 eggs
1 cup white corn syrup
1 teaspoon vanilla extract
1/2 cup sugar

1 cup chopped pecans
1/2 teaspoon salt
1 (9 inch) pie shell

In a large bowl, beat eggs until foamy. Add syrup, vanilla and blend well. Fold in sugar, pecans, and salt. Mix well. Pour mixture into pie shell. Bake in a 350° oven for 50 minutes or until golden brown. Remove from oven and cool on a wire rack. Yields 8 slices.

GINGER BREAD

2 ½ cups all-purpose flour
¾ teaspoon baking soda
½ teaspoon salt
1 teaspoon ground allspice
1 teaspoon ground cinnamon
1 teaspoon ground cloves

½ teaspoon ground ginger
1 cup packed light brown sugar
¼ cup margarine, softened
2 eggs
1 cup water
1 cup molasses

In a medium bowl, combine flour, soda, salt, and spices; mix well and set aside. Cream sugar and butter in a large bowl. Beat in eggs one at a time. Bring water to a boil in a small saucepan; remove from heat and stir in molasses. Add to creamed mixture alternately with dry ingredients and mix well. Pour into a greased 13 x 9 x 2 inch baking pan and bake in a 350° oven for 30 minutes, or until a toothpick inserted in center comes out clean. Cool slightly and cut into squares. Serve warm. Yields 12 servings.

BANANA DROP COOKIES

1 ½ cups sugar
⅔ cup margarine
1 teaspoon vanilla extract
2 eggs
1 cup mashed bananas
2 ¼ cups all-purpose flour

2 teaspoons baking powder
¼ teaspoon baking soda
½ teaspoon salt
1 cup chopped nuts
1 teaspoon cinnamon

In a large bowl, cream 1¼ cups sugar (reserve remainder), margarine, and vanilla until light and fluffy. Add eggs and beat well. Stir in mashed bananas, flour, baking powder, baking soda, and salt. Mix well. Stir in nuts. Chill mixture for 30 minutes in refrigerator. Drop by teaspoonful on greased baking sheet 2 inches apart. Mix remaining sugar and cinnamon and sprinkle over cookie dough. Bake at 400° for 8 to 10 minutes, or until light brown. Yields 5 dozen cookies.

9

OBBIE'S CAJUN COOKIES

¾ cup margarine

1½ cups sugar

3 eggs

3½ cups all-purpose flour

2 teaspoons cinnamon

1 pound raisins

3 cups chopped pecans

1 teaspoon baking soda

⅛ cup boiling water

In a large bowl, cream together margarine and sugar; add eggs and blend well. In another bowl, combine flour, cinnamon, raisins, and pecans. Mix thoroughly. In a measuring cup dissolve baking soda in water. Add to flour mixture. Pour sugar mixture into flour mixture and mix well. Drop by teaspoonful on greased baking sheet. Bake at 375° until brown. Store in tightly–closed container. Yields 7 to 8 dozen cookies.

PAGE BOY COOKIES

1 teaspoon baking soda

4 tablespoons boiling water

4½ cups all-purpose flour

½ teaspoon salt

2½ cups sugar

8 tablespoons butter

2 eggs

½ cup cane syrup

2 teaspoons vanilla extract

1 cup chopped nuts

In a measuring cup, dissolve soda in water. In a large bowl, sift flour with salt. In a separate bowl, cream together sugar and butter. Add eggs and blend well. Add soda mixture to flour mixture. Mix well. Pour egg mixture into flour mixture; add syrup, vanilla, and nuts. Blend well. Form in a roll, wrap in waxed paper, and chill overnight. Slice and place on cookie sheet. Bake 10 minutes in a 325° oven. Dough may be frozen. Yields 4 dozen cookies.

These cookies are very crisp. Keep them in a tightly-closed container to retain their crispness.

APPLE CAKE

2 cups sugar
1 cup shortening
4 eggs
1 teaspoon vanilla extract
1/2 cup bourbon or sherry wine
3 cups all-purpose flour
1/2 teaspoon salt
1 teaspoon baking powder

1 teaspoon baking soda
1 teaspoon cinnamon
1 teaspoon nutmeg
3 cups grated or cubed apples
1 cup chopped dates
  (or white raisins)
2 cups chopped pecans

In a large bowl, cream together the sugar and shortening. Beat eggs in, one at a time. Add vanilla. In a separate bowl mix dry ingredients and add to the liquid mixture, using bourbon to thin. Add apples, dates, and nuts. Bake in Bundt pan at 350° for 1 hour. Yields 12 servings.

APPLE PECAN CAKE

3 eggs
2 cups sugar
1 cup oil
2 teaspoons vanilla extract
2 3/4 cups all-purpose flour

1 teaspoon baking soda
1 teaspoon salt
2 teaspoons cinnamon
4 cups peeled, chopped apples
1 cup chopped pecans

In a large mixing bowl, beat eggs at medium speed with an electric mixer until thick and pale. Gradually add sugar, beating until blended. Add oil and vanilla; beat at low speed until blended. In a separate bowl, combine flour, baking soda, salt, and cinnamon; add to egg mixture, stirring until blended. Stir in apples and pecans. Pour batter into a greased and floured 10 inch tube pan. Bake at 350° for 1 hour and 25 minutes or until a toothpick inserted in the center comes out clean. Cool cake in pan on a wire rack for 5 minutes; remove from pan and cool completely on wire rack. Yields 12 servings.

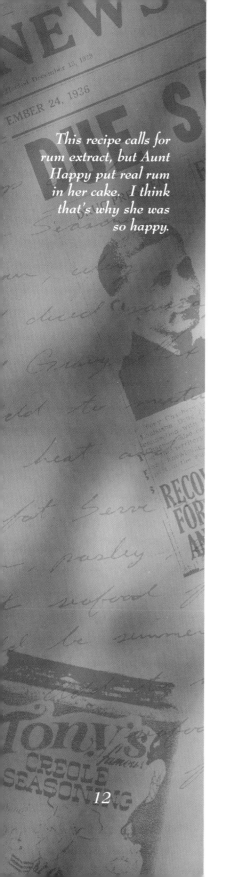

This recipe calls for rum extract, but Aunt Happy put real rum in her cake. I think that's why she was so happy.

AUNT HAPPY'S CAKE

2 sticks margarine, softened
2 1/2 cups sugar
5 eggs
1 1/2 teaspoons coconut extract

1 1/2 teaspoons rum extract
3 cups cake flour
1 teaspoon baking powder
1 cup milk

In a bowl, cream margarine and sugar together. Add eggs, one at a time, beating well. Add coconut and rum extracts. In a larger bowl, sift flour with baking powder, add milk and stir. Pour egg mixture into large bowl and blend well. Pour into greased and floured tube pan. Start in a cold oven. Set at 350° and bake 1 hour. This makes two small Bundt cakes or one large tube cake. Yields 24 servings.

Glaze for Cake

1 cup sugar
1/2 cup water

1 teaspoon almond extract

In a pot, mix sugar with water. Bring to a boil and cook for 5 minutes. Add almond extract and pour glaze over cake.

FIG CAKE

1 cup sugar
1/2 cup oil
8 tablespoons butter
1 cup boiling water
2 eggs
2 cups all-purpose flour

2 teaspoons baking soda
1 teaspoon vanilla extract
1 tablespoon cinnamon
1 pint fig preserves
1 cup chopped pecans

In a large bowl, mix sugar, oil, butter, and boiling water. Add remaining ingredients and blend well. Bake in 9 x 12 inch greased dish at 350° for 1 hour. Yields 12 servings.

PINEAPPLE CAKE

8 tablespoons butter
2 cups sugar
3 cups all-purpose flour
3 teaspoons baking powder

1 cup milk
4 eggs
1 (20 oz.) can crushed
    pineapple, drained

In a large bowl, cream together butter and sugar. Sift flour with baking powder, and add alternately with milk. Beat in one egg at a time. Bake in four 8 inch pans in a 350° oven for 25 to 30 minutes until lightly brown and cake tester comes out clean. Spread crushed pineapple between layers. Yields 12 servings.

Cream Cheese Icing

1 (3 oz.) package cream cheese
4 tablespoons butter, softened
2 tablespoons cream
1 tablespoon lemon juice

3 teaspoons grated lemon rind
1 teaspoon vanilla extract
4 cups sifted confectioners sugar

In a bowl, combine all ingredients and beat until light and fluffy. Spread over cooled cake.

13

This one goes way back.
So good with a big
glass of milk.

GATEAU DE SIROP
Cajun Syrup Cake

½ cup shortening
1½ cups molasses
2 eggs
2½ cups all-purpose flour
1 teaspoon cinnamon
1 teaspoon allspice

2 teaspoons ginger
¼ teaspoon salt
1 cup raisins
1¼ teaspoons baking soda
1 cup boiling water

In a bowl, dredge raisins with a little flour and set aside. In a another bowl, cream shortening and molasses. Beat in eggs one at a time. In a third bowl, combine flour, cinnamon, allspice, ginger and salt. Add raisins to flour mixture. Pour molasses mixture into flour mixture. In a large measuring cup, dissolve baking soda in boiling water and add to mixture. Stir until smooth. Pour into greased and floured oblong baking pan and bake at 350° until cake comes away from sides of the pan (about 30 minutes). Yields 12 servings.

RIZ AU LAIT
Louisiana Rice Pudding

1 cup uncooked rice
1 quart milk
8 tablespoons butter
¾ cup sugar

1 teaspoon vanilla extract
½ cup raisins
5 eggs, beaten
½ teaspoon cinnamon

Combine rice and milk. Bring to a boil; cover and cook over low heat until rice is tender and has absorbed most of the milk. Add butter, sugar, vanilla, raisins, and eggs. Turn into a buttered 2 quart casserole. Sprinkle with cinnamon. Bake at 350° for 25 minutes. Yields 6 servings.

BANANA NUT BREAD

4 tablespoons margarine, softened
1 cup sugar
2 ripe bananas, mashed
1 tablespoon baking soda
2 tablespoons boiling water

2 eggs, slightly beaten
1 teaspoon lemon juice
1/2 cup chopped pecans
2 cups all-purpose flour
Cooking spray

In a bowl, cream margarine and sugar until light and fluffy. Add bananas. In a measuring cup dissolve soda in water. Add dissolved soda, eggs, lemon juice, pecans, and flour to sugar mixture; stir. Pour batter into a loaf pan coated with cooking spray. Bake in a 350° oven for 1 hour or until center is cooked. Remove from oven and cool on wire rack. Serve warm or cooled. Yields 12 slices.

BANANA SPLIT DESSERT

2 cups graham cracker crumbs
6 tablespoons margarine, melted
2 (3½ oz.) packages instant
vanilla pudding mix
2 cups milk

3 bananas, sliced
1 (20 oz.) can crushed
    pineapple, drained
1 (12 oz.) container
    whipped topping

In a bowl, combine crumbs and margarine. Press mixture into an oblong baking dish and set aside. In another bowl, prepare pudding mix with milk according to package directions. Spread pudding over crumb mixture. Layer with banana slices, then pineapple, then whipped topping. Chill 3 hours or overnight. Cut into squares to serve. Yields 12 squares.

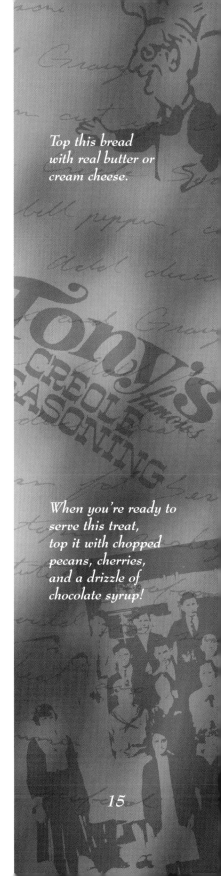

Top this bread with real butter or cream cheese.

When you're ready to serve this treat, top it with chopped pecans, cherries, and a drizzle of chocolate syrup!

15

CROQUESIGNOLES AND COFFEE MILK

My Mama's favorite breakfast treats for us kids were croquesignoles. They were the country folks' version of the city folks' beignets. They're much like doughnuts, except the dough is heavier and they're never cut into a perfect ring!

Croquesignoles are squares of pastry dough, punctured with a fork to make a couple of long holes. They're fried in oil then coated with sugar and cinnamon.

We looked forward to the treat as kids because she served it with cafe au lait or "coffee milk." Most kids don't drink coffee today, but down here we're probably addicted to it because we had it as young as five!

Nowadays, I fix 'em with powdered sugar and I still love 'em with sweetened coffee milk.

BEIGNETS
OR CROQUESIGNOLES

2 cups self-rising flour
2 tablespoons sugar
Pinch of salt
1 egg

1 1/4 cups milk
Oil for frying
Confectioners sugar

In a bowl, blend dry ingredients. In another bowl, blend egg
and milk; add to dry mixture. Beat to a thick batter. Drop by
tablespoonful into oil heated to 375°. Deep fry until golden brown.
Drain on absorbent paper. Sprinkle with confectioners sugar.
Yields 30 beignets or 18 croquesignoles.

PEPPER JELLY

1/2 cup hot red or green peppers
1 1/2 cups finely chopped
  bell peppers
6 1/2 cups sugar

1 1/2 cups wine vinegar
1 small bottle Certo
3 or 4 tablespoons red or
  green food coloring, optional

Seed and finely chop hot peppers. In a large pot, mix peppers with
sugar and vinegar. Bring to a boil. Boil 2 minutes. Reduce heat
and cook 5 minutes longer, then add Certo and food coloring. Pour
into jelly jars. Yields four 4 oz. jars.

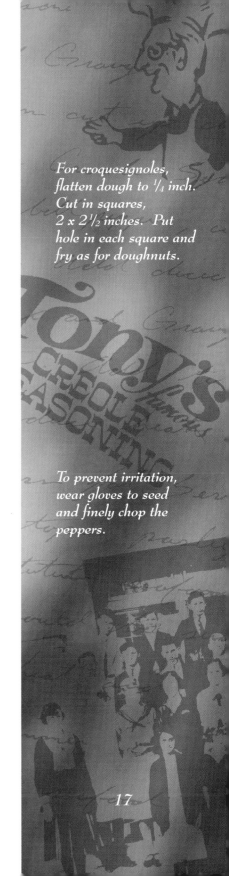

For croquesignoles,
flatten dough to 1/4 inch.
Cut in squares,
2 x 2 1/2 inches. Put
hole in each square and
fry as for doughnuts.

To prevent irritation,
wear gloves to seed
and finely chop the
peppers.

17

Wear gloves while chopping hot peppers to prevent skin irritation.

Most folks I know keep their jar of chow chow on the kitchen table, next to their shaker of my seasoning!

GREEN TOMATO RELISH

8 cups chopped green tomatoes	*2 cups sugar*
4 cups chopped onions	*4 cups vinegar*
1 cup chopped hot peppers	*Tony's Creole Seasoning*

In a pot, mix ingredients and bring to a boil. Use firm green tomatoes and start canning as soon as the mixture begins to boil to prevent tomatoes from softening. Yields 8 pints.

CHOW CHOW

4 cucumbers	*3 cloves garlic*
6 green tomatoes	*4 bell peppers*
2 onions	

Chop above ingredients or grind coarsely. Place in a pot and add:

4 cups vinegar	*3 teaspoons pickling spice*
2 cups sugar	

Cook slowly for 1 hour until thick. Put immediately in hot, sterilized jars and seal. Yields 4 pints.

FOUR-DAY
SWEET PICKLES

8 pounds cucumbers
1 cup salt
3 tablespoons alum
2 gallons water

1 teaspoon ginger
1/2 gallon vinegar
5 pounds sugar
1 bag pickling spice

Slice cucumbers thin. In a large container, submerge in salt water for 3 days. Wash and drain; place in mixture of alum and 1 gallon water. Let stand 1 day. Drain water and rinse. In a stock pot, place cucumbers, ginger, and 1 gallon water; bring to a hard boil. Drain water and rinse. In stock pot, make a syrup of vinegar, sugar, and pickling spice. Bring to a boil. Add cucumbers and boil for 3 minutes. Pack and seal in hot jars. Yields 8 pints.

FRENCH OMELET

2 tablespoons margarine
4 eggs
1/3 cup heavy cream
Dash of hot pepper sauce
Crumbled bacon or ham bits
Tony's Creole Seasoning
1 tablespoon finely chopped
  green onions

1/4 cup chopped red and green
  peppers
1 tablespoon pimiento bits
1/4 cup sliced mushrooms
1/4 cup stewed tomatoes,
  drained (optional)

Melt margarine in omelet pan. In a large bowl, beat eggs. Add cream, hot pepper sauce, bacon bits, and Tony's Creole Seasoning. Add vegetables. Stir. Reduce heat under margarine and pour one–half of the mixture into the pan. Lift edges gently with a spatula to let liquid run down into the pan as the omelet cooks. Omelet should be creamy inside. Raise heat for 1 minute to brown bottom quickly; fold over and slide out of pan. Repeat process with other half of mixture for second omelet. Yields 2 servings.

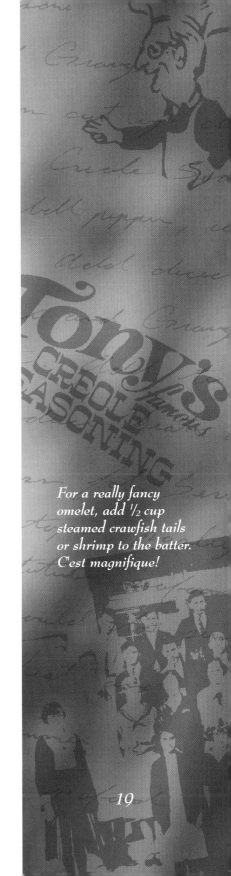

For a really fancy omelet, add 1/2 cup steamed crawfish tails or shrimp to the batter. C'est magnifique!

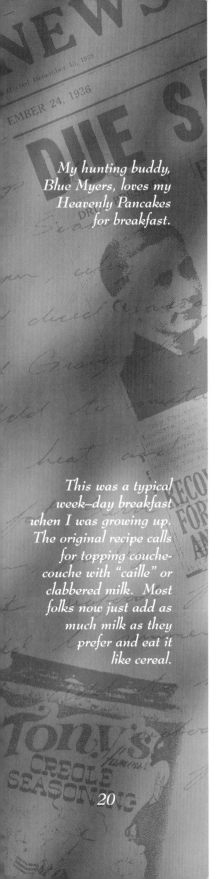

My hunting buddy, Blue Myers, loves my Heavenly Pancakes for breakfast.

TONY'S HEAVENLY PANCAKES

1 cup all-purpose flour
2 teaspoons baking powder
1 tablespoon sugar
½ teaspoon salt

2 tablespoons melted butter
2 eggs, well beaten
¾ cup Half and Half cream

In a bowl, mix flour, baking powder, sugar, and salt. In a larger bowl, combine melted butter, eggs, and cream. Mix well. Add dry mixture and stir just enough to get an even mixture. If too thick, add more cream so that batter pours easily. Ladle onto a hot, greased griddle. When bubbles form, turn over and cook the other side. Serve with butter and fig preserves and a glass of milk. Yields 2 servings.

COUCHE-COUCHE

This was a typical week-day breakfast when I was growing up. The original recipe calls for topping couche-couche with "caille" or clabbered milk. Most folks now just add as much milk as they prefer and eat it like cereal.

2 cups corn meal
1 teaspoon baking powder
1 teaspoon salt

1½ cups milk
½ cup pan drippings or
   margarine

In a bowl, mix thoroughly corn meal, baking powder, salt, and milk. In a heavy skillet, heat pan drippings and add corn meal mixture. Stir. Lower heat; cover and cook for 15 minutes, stirring often. When a crust is formed on the bottom, stir and serve in cereal bowls and cover with milk. Yields 12 servings

PAIN PERDU
Lost Bread

2 eggs
1 cup sugar
1 teaspoon vanilla extract
2 cups milk

$\frac{1}{2}$ teaspoon cinnamon
8 slices white bread
Margarine
Confectioners sugar

In a large bowl, beat eggs well; add sugar and continue to beat. Add vanilla, milk, and cinnamon. Mix well. Dip bread slices in mixture, coating each side thoroughly. Use just enough margarine to cover the bottom of a skillet and fry over moderate heat. Fry each side of the bread until golden brown. Serve hot, sprinkled with confectioners sugar. Yields 4 servings.

GRILLADES

1 pound pork steaks
Tony's Creole Seasoning
$\frac{1}{2}$ cup vinegar

Cooking spray
2 tablespoons chopped onion

Cut steaks in 2 inch pieces. Season with Tony's Creole Seasoning. Place in a jar, add vinegar, and refrigerate overnight. When ready to cook, place drained grillades (pork pieces) in a skillet coated with cooking spray and brown on each side. Add onion, water to cover, and simmer for 1 hour. Yields 4 servings.

Also called French toast, this popular breakfast or brunch treat is still a favorite in south Louisiana.

Grillades are traditionally served over grits. Great for Sunday brunch!

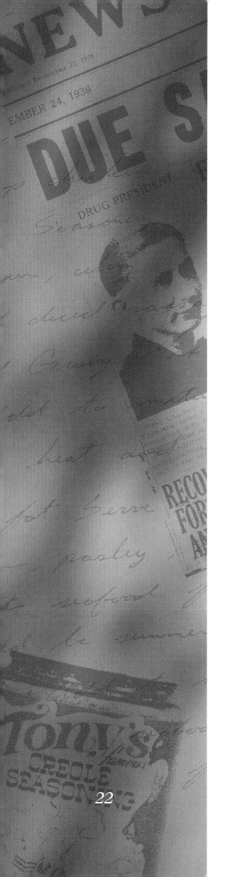

CREOLE
SMOTHERED LIVER

1 pound calf liver
3 cups boiling water
Tony's Creole Seasoning
½ cup all-purpose flour

2 tablespoons oil
1 cup hot water
1 tablespoon chopped green
  onions

Cut liver in thin slices. Dip in boiling water for an instant; drain and make a few gashes in each side. Sprinkle with Tony's Creole Seasoning and roll in flour. Shake off excess flour. In a skillet fry liver in oil for 5 minutes, turning once. Add hot water and green onions. Reduce heat, cover skillet and smother for 5 minutes or until tender. Do not over cook. Serve with grits. Yields 4 servings.

OLD-FASHIONED
BUTTERMILK BISCUITS

2 cups all–purpose flour, sifted
½ teaspoon salt
½ teaspoon baking soda
3 teaspoons baking powder

2 tablespoons shortening
1 cup buttermilk
¼ cup melted butter

Combine flour, salt, baking soda, and baking powder in mixing bowl and cut in shortening until fine. Add buttermilk, stirring briskly until mixed. Turn onto floured board; knead gently several times. Form into ball; pat out ¼ inch thick. Spread with half of the butter. Fold over, forming two layers. Brush top with remaining butter. Cut into rounds with floured biscuit cutter. Place ½ inch apart in buttered 9 inch pan. Bake at 400° 12 to 15 minutes. Yields 12 large biscuits.

TONY'S OLD-FASHIONED CREOLE CORN BREAD

2 cups yellow corn meal
1 cup all-purpose flour
1 cup sour cream
3 teaspoons baking powder
½ cup sugar

2 eggs
1 cup cream style corn
1½ teaspoons salt
½ cup bacon drippings
Milk

In a large bowl, mix all ingredients together, except milk; stir until well blended. Add enough milk to make the mixture pour easily. Spoon into greased muffin tins or baking pan. Bake in 400° oven for 20 to 30 minutes or until golden brown. Yields 8 servings.

SAUSAGE CORN BREAD

1 pound pork sausage, chopped
1 cup corn meal
½ cup all-purpose flour
2 teaspoons baking powder
Pinch of salt

¾ cup milk
1 egg
3 tablespoons shortening
2 tablespoons sugar

Cook pork sausage in a heavy iron skillet until slightly brown. Pour off excess fat. In a large bowl, combine remaining ingredients and mix well. Place sausage in square baking pan, then pour in corn bread mixture. Bake in 425° oven for 20 minutes or until light brown. Yields 10 servings.

Serve with butter and pure cane syrup, and sop your way to the Promised Land!

23

LEARNING TO COOK

Back in 1929, I made my first trip to Intracoastal City, a place not yet on the map, but most folks knew it was south of Abbeville. The fishing party that day included my brother-in-law Grady Martin from Crowley, his father, and me. We fished at the point where the fresh water met the salt water in Vermilion Bay. Grady caught a gaspergou, not good for broiling or stuffing, but mighty fine for stewing.

Back at the fishing camp, Grady's father used the "goo" to make a "courtbouillon"-- something new to me. Its taste was out of this world! I vowed to go home and try this myself. I asked Grady's father how long the goo needed cooking. "Oh, 'bout twenty minutes," he said.

My first try was quite a disaster. I had chopped vegetables, made a roux, cleaned the fish, and stirred this altogether over a fire for twenty minutes. I ended up with a tasteless pot of undercooked goo-lash!

Grady's father had been "pulling my leg." I'll never forget it. I vowed to do it over and get it right. That day my desire to be a culinarian was born.

Some time later, I joined a few fellows for a fishing weekend at Second Lake, bag of vegetables in tow. My buddies and I caught a nice mess of fish for my first masterpiece courtbouillon. That day the ingredients took their sweet old time cooking in the old black iron pot on the hearth. I was patient...my patience paid off. I've been cooking ever since.

BASIC VEGETABLE MIXTURE

1 onion	2 ribs celery
1/2 bell pepper	1 clove garlic

Put vegetables through meat grinder or blender. Yields 1 cup.

TONY'S RED SAUCE

4 tablespoons margarine	1 teaspoon lemon juice
1 (8 oz.) can tomato sauce	2 cups basic vegetable mixture
1/2 teaspoon sugar	4 cups water
1 teaspoon Worcestershire sauce	Tony's Creole Seasoning

Melt margarine in a heavy saucepan; add tomato sauce and sugar. Cook 5 minutes. Add all other ingredients. Simmer for 2 hours or until thick. Add more water if needed and season with Tony's Creole Seasoning. Yields 4 cups.

ROUX

1 cup oil or margarine	1 cup all-purpose flour

Heat oil in a heavy pot. When the oil is hot, gradually add the flour, stirring continuously until well mixed. Lower heat and continue stirring until chocolate brown. Remove from pot and set aside. If roux remains in the pot, it will continue to cook and get too dark. Always use warm water to dissolve the roux.

Some folks call onion, bell pepper and celery the "Cajun Trinity." I say garlic's always got to be in the mix. I never cook a meal without this basic vegetable mixture.

For Italian dishes, add different herbs or cheese to the sauce.

For fish dishes, add mushrooms, shrimp or crab meat to the sauce.

If you're watching calories or fat, try my fat-free Tony's Roux and Gravy Mix. It can be substituted in any recipe which calls for roux.

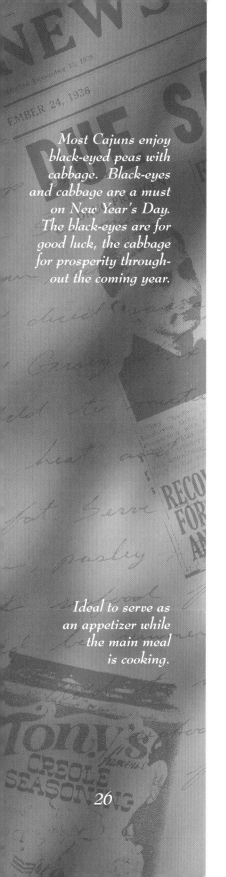

Most Cajuns enjoy black-eyed peas with cabbage. Black-eyes and cabbage are a must on New Year's Day. The black-eyes are for good luck, the cabbage for prosperity through-out the coming year.

BLACK-EYED PEAS

1 pound black-eyed peas
3 quarts water
1 cup chopped onions
1 bell pepper, chopped
½ cup chopped parsley
2 bay leaves

1 teaspoon basil
Tony's Creole Seasoning
Ham bone
1 pound smoked sausage,
  cut in ½ inch slices

In a medium pot, soak peas overnight in enough water to cover. Drain and rinse. Place all ingredients, except the sausage, in a heavy pot and cook for 1 hour. Meanwhile, brown the sausage in a skillet, and drain. Add sausage to the beans and continue cooking until creamy. Add a little oil for creaminess when lean ham or pork is used.

Any kind of pork may be substituted for the sausage, including ham, salt meat, pickled pork, or andouille. Black-eyed peas are usually served over rice. However, a soup may be made of black-eyed peas, red beans, or white beans. Yields 6 servings.

TONY'S PINTO BEANS AND SMOKED HAM HOCKS

1 (2 lb.) package pinto beans
4 smoked ham hocks
2 large onions, chopped
1 bell pepper, chopped

6 cloves garlic, minced
Tony's Creole Seasoning
1 tablespoon Worcestershire
  sauce

In a medium pot, soak beans overnight in enough water to cover. Drain and rinse. Using a 5 quart pot, add all ingredients with sufficient water to cover; bring to a boil. Reduce heat and simmer slowly until meat falls from the bones and beans are tender (about 1 hour). Remove bones and fat. Adjust seasoning; continue to simmer until sauce is thick. Yields 20 small servings.

Ideal to serve as an appetizer while the main meal is cooking.

26

RED BEANS AND RICE

3 cups dried red beans
1 tablespoon oil
1 tablespoon all-purpose flour
1 onion, chopped
1 garlic clove, minced

1 ham bone with plenty of
    meat or 1 pound smoked
    sausage
Tony's Creole Seasoning
4 green onions, minced

In a medium pot, soak beans overnight in enough water to cover.
Drain and rinse. Heat oil in deep pot over low heat. Add flour,
onions, and garlic. Stir frequently and cook until light brown. Add
ham bone and beans. Add enough water to cover the beans. Season
with Tony's Creole Seasoning. Cook slowly until beans are tender
(about 1 hour), stirring often. Serve over steamed rice and garnish
with green onions. Yields 6 servings.

TURNIP GREENS
COOKED WITH TASSO

4 bundles turnips
2 tablespoons margarine

1/2 pound tasso

Cut off turnip bottoms; peel and dice. Pick tender parts of turnip
leaves away from stems and tough veins. Wash thoroughly more than
once. Put margarine and tasso in a large heavy pot and heat well. Add
washed greens, but no extra water. Cook 30 minutes.

Halfway through cooking the greens, add the diced turnips and cook
until tender.

Mustard greens, chard, kale, or any other greens may be cooked in
the same manner. Serve with corn bread to sop up all the flavor!
Yields 8 servings.

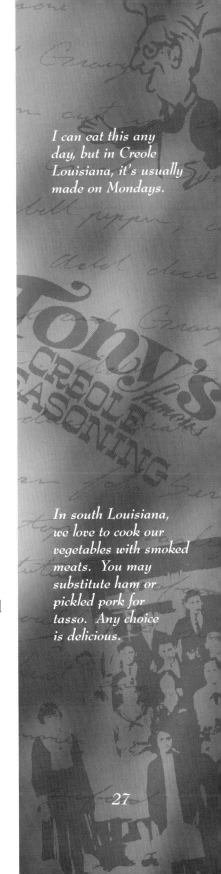

I can eat this any
day, but in Creole
Louisiana, it's usually
made on Mondays.

In south Louisiana,
we love to cook our
vegetables with smoked
meats. You may
substitute ham or
pickled pork for
tasso. Any choice
is delicious.

27

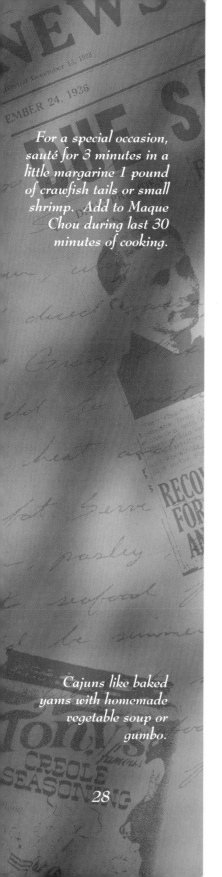

For a special occasion, sauté for 3 minutes in a little margarine 1 pound of crawfish tails or small shrimp. Add to Maque Chou during last 30 minutes of cooking.

MAQUE CHOU

12 ears tender fresh corn
4 tablespoons margarine
1 onion, chopped
1 bell pepper, chopped

1 clove garlic, minced
1 tomato, diced
Tony's Creole Seasoning
1 cup milk

In a large bowl, cut corn off cob and scrape cobs to get all the juice; set aside. Heat margarine in a Dutch oven; add onion, bell pepper, and garlic. Sauté until tender. Add corn, tomato, and Tony's Creole Seasoning. Cook mixture over medium heat for 1 hour, stirring often. Add a little milk from time to time to keep mixture soft. Yields 12 servings as a side dish.

Chicken Maque Chou

1 (3 lb.) fryer, cut up
Tony's Creole Seasoning
1 egg, well beaten

1 cup milk
1 cup all-purpose flour
Oil to fry

Season chicken and set aside. In a bowl, combine egg and milk. Dip chicken in egg mixture; dredge in flour and shake off excess. Fry in oil until cooked; add to Maque Chou. Simmer 5 minutes. Serve over steamed rice. Yields 6 servings as a entree.

BAKED GOLDEN LOUISIANA YAMS

Cajuns like baked yams with homemade vegetable soup or gumbo.

12 yams

1/4 cup oil

Wash and dry yams thoroughly. Do not remove skins. Rub skins with oil and place in open baking pan. Bake in a 400° oven for 2 hours or until tender. Peel and serve with your favorite meal or eat as is. Yields 12 servings.

SWEET POTATO PONE

4 cups peeled, grated sweet potato
4 tablespoons margarine
1/2 teaspoon cinnamon
Grated rind of 1 orange
Juice of 1 orange

3/4 cup sugar
1/4 teaspoon salt
1/2 cup milk
1 egg
1/4 teaspoon nutmeg

In a bowl, mix all ingredients together. Bake in a shallow dish at 350° for 1 hour or until set. May be served hot or cold. Yields 12 servings.

POTATO SALAD

5 pounds potatoes
8 eggs
1/2 cup mayonnaise

3 tablespoons Creole mustard
Tony's Creole Seasoning
Paprika

Peel potatoes and cut into large chunks. In a large pot, boil eggs and potatoes for 20 minutes (a little longer if potatoes are still hard). Place potatoes in a large bowl. Peel eggs and extract the yolks. In another bowl, mash yolks and mix with mayonnaise and mustard until creamy. Chop egg whites and place in the bowl with potatoes. Add yolk mixture and blend well. Season with Tony's Creole Seasoning. Serve warm immediately or chill and serve cold. Garnish with a sprinkle of paprika. Yields 10 servings.

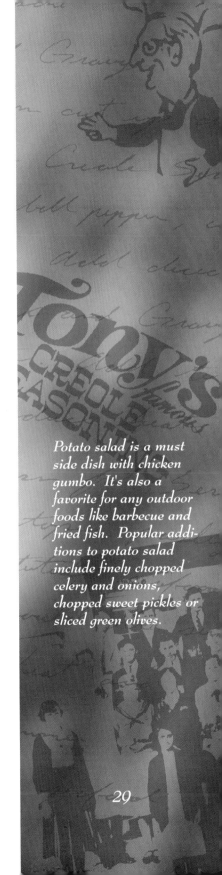

Potato salad is a must side dish with chicken gumbo. It's also a favorite for any outdoor foods like barbecue and fried fish. Popular additions to potato salad include finely chopped celery and onions, chopped sweet pickles or sliced green olives.

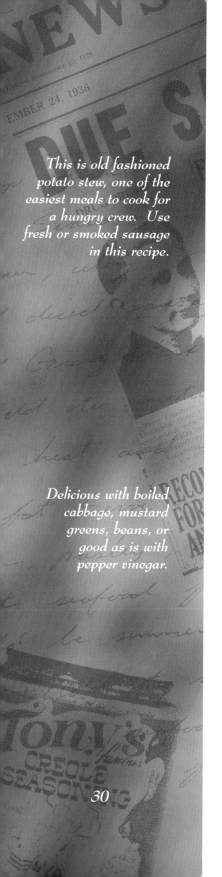

SAUCE DE POMME DE TERRE

2 pounds sausage
5 pounds potatoes, peeled
  and cut in chunks
1 bell pepper, chopped

2 onions, chopped
3 ribs celery, chopped
Tony's Creole Seasoning

Chop sausage into ½ inch slices and brown in a Dutch oven on medium heat. Add potatoes, and chopped vegetables. Sauté until light brown. Add 1 inch of water, reduce heat and simmer about 20 minutes. Allow potatoes to begin to break apart to thicken gravy. Add Tony's Creole Seasoning. Yields 8 servings.

CREOLE SALT PORK
Viande Salee

From a fresh picnic shoulder ham, cut pieces of pork 2 inches thick, 6 inches long, and 4 inches wide. In a crock, place a layer of coarse salt and then a layer of meat. Cover the meat with another layer of salt. Continue this process until all meat is used and all meat is covered with salt. Cover crock with muslin.

Place in cool spot (not in refrigerator) until salt is melted and all meat is covered with brine (takes from 2 to 3 weeks). Remove from crock, wash in warm water, dry and store in refrigerator. Use as needed to add in the cooking of other foods.

FRIED OKRA

24 okra pods, 4 inches or shorter   Cracker crumbs
Tony's Creole Seasoning   Oil, for frying
1 egg, beaten

Wash okra, drain. Season with Tony's Creole Seasoning. Roll the
pods in the egg, then in cracker crumbs. Deep fry in hot oil until
delicate brown. Drain on absorbent paper and serve as hot as
possible. Yields 4 servings.

SMOTHERED OKRA
AND TOMATOES

2 pounds okra   ½ bell pepper, chopped
3 tablespoons oil   2 ribs celery, chopped
1 tablespoon all-purpose flour   5 tomatoes, chopped
1 onion, chopped   Tony's Creole Seasoning

Wash okra. Cut in ⅛ inch slices. Fry in an aluminum pot on
medium heat in 2 tablespoons oil until okra is no longer sticky.

In another skillet, make a medium dark roux with 1 tablespoon oil
and flour. Add onion, bell pepper, and celery. Simmer until tender.
Add tomatoes and simmer for 5 minutes. Add okra, seasoned with
Tony's Creole Seasoning. Simmer for 1 hour. Yields 6 servings.

Can be frozen for later use. Ideal for gumbo.

31

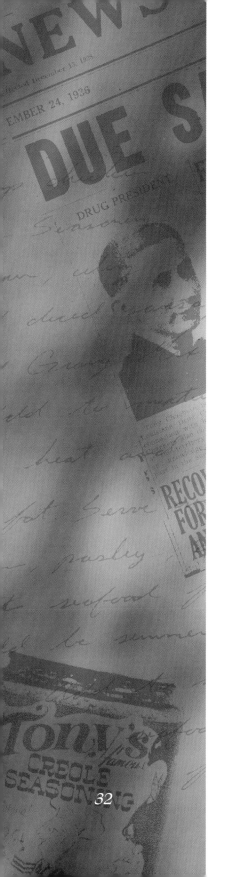

CREOLE
VEGETABLE SOUP

1 (2 lb.) beef brisket, or
  soup bone
2 ribs celery
1 onion
1 potato
3 quarts water
1 (20 oz.) can tomatoes
1 cup chopped cabbage
3 carrots, chopped
2 ribs celery, chopped

$\frac{1}{2}$ onion, chopped
$\frac{1}{2}$ potato, chopped
2 sprigs parsley, minced
1 (15 oz.) can whole kernel corn
1 turnip, diced
2 tablespoons rice
Small amount broken
  spaghetti or macaroni
Tony's Creole Seasoning

In a 4 quart covered pot, boil meat in seasoned water with whole ribs of celery, whole onion, and whole potato. Simmer for 3 hours. Take soup meat from pot and remove meat from bone. Chop meat into bite–size pieces, discarding bone and fat.

Mash cooked celery, onion, and potato through a strainer. Return these ingredients to the pot along with the meat. Add all other vegetables and rice; cook until vegetables are tender. Break small amount of spaghetti or macaroni into soup during last 20 minutes of cooking. Season with Tony's Creole Seasoning. Yields 10 servings.

CHICKEN SOUP

1 (3 lb.) fryer, cut up
Tony's Creole Seasoning
5 quarts water
1 onion, finely chopped
4 cloves garlic, finely chopped
3 ribs celery, finely chopped

1/2 bell pepper, finely chopped
2 or 3 medium potatoes, diced
2 or 3 carrots, diced
1/4 cup finely chopped parsley
6 ounces curly vermicelli or egg
   pastina

Remove skin and all visible fat from chicken. Wash, drain, and season with Tony's Creole Seasoning. In a large stock pot, add water and boil chicken with onion, garlic, celery, and bell pepper until chicken is tender. Remove chicken from pot and let cool. Skim fat from soup. Add potatoes and carrots. Debone chicken and return to soup. Add parsley and cook until carrots and potatoes are tender. In a separate pot, cook pasta. Drain and add a small amount of soup to prevent sticking. Add pasta to the soup as it is served. Yields 8 servings.

CREOLE BOUILLI

1 cup oil
1 cup all-purpose flour
4 onions, chopped
1 bell pepper, chopped
4 ribs celery, chopped
4 cloves garlic, minced
5 pounds bouilli meat (calf
   kidney, heart, melt,
   sweetbreads, and brisket),
   cut in small pieces

2 (20 oz.) cans tomatoes
1 cup diced potatoes
1 (15 oz.) can whole kernel corn
1 (6 oz.) can tomato paste
1 teaspoon sugar
4 quarts water
Tony's Creole Seasoning

In a large pot make a dark roux with oil and flour. Add vegetables and cook 5 minutes. Add meat; mix well. Add all other ingredients. Season with Tony's Creole Seasoning. Cook for 4 hours, adding more water as necessary. Serve over steamed rice. Yields 10 servings.

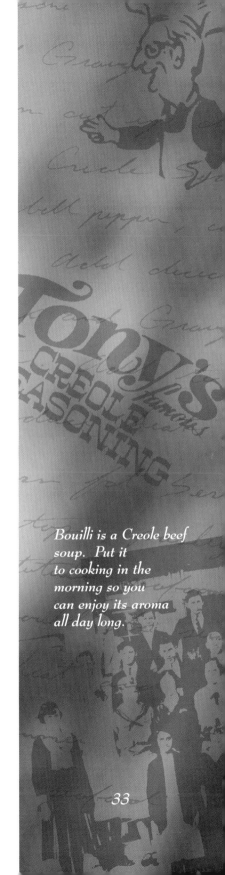

Bouilli is a Creole beef soup. Put it to cooking in the morning so you can enjoy its aroma all day long.

33

To save time, potatoes can also be cooked in the microwave (about 12 minutes).

BAKED POTATO SOUP

4 potatoes
4 tablespoons margarine
⅔ cup all-purpose flour
6 cups milk
Tony's Creole Seasoning
4 green onions, chopped

12 slices bacon, cooked, crumbled
1¼ cups shredded Cheddar cheese
1 (8 oz.) carton sour cream

Wash potatoes and prick several times with a fork; bake at 400° for 1 hour or until cooked. Let cool. Cut potatoes in half lengthwise; scoop out pulp and set aside in a bowl. Discard skins. Melt margarine in a heavy saucepan over low heat; add flour, stirring until smooth. Cook 1 minute, stirring constantly. Gradually add milk; cook over medium heat, stirring constantly, until mixture is thickened and bubbly. Add potato pulp, Tony's Creole Seasoning, 2 tablespoons green onions, ½ cup bacon, and 1 cup cheese. Cook until thoroughly heated. Stir in sour cream. Add extra milk, if necessary, for desired consistency. Serve with remaining green onions, bacon, and cheese. Yields 12 servings.

SOUTHERN CHICKEN PIE

5 tablespoons margarine
1 onion, chopped
4 tablespoons all-purpose flour
2 cups chicken broth
Tony's Creole Seasoning

2½ cups cooked chicken pieces
2 cups diced ham
1 large can biscuit dough

Melt margarine over low heat in a heavy pan; add onions and cook until transparent. Add flour and stir until blended. Slowly add chicken broth and stir over low heat until thick and smooth. Season with Tony's Creole Seasoning. Arrange chicken meat in layers with diced ham in a large casserole, or in 6 ramekins. Cover with sauce. Top with biscuit dough, toasted bread crumbs, or pastry. Bake in 350° oven for 20 minutes. Yields 6 servings.

34

SHRIMP AND OKRA GUMBO

2 cups fresh okra, diced
6 tablespoons oil
4 tablespoons all-purpose flour
1 bell pepper, chopped
2 ribs celery, chopped
2 cloves garlic, minced
1 onion, chopped

3 quarts water
2 pounds shrimp, peeled
Tony's Creole Seasoning
3 tablespoon chopped green
  onions
Filé

In an aluminum Dutch oven, fry okra in 2 tablespoons oil for 10 minutes, stirring constantly to prevent burning. Remove okra and set aside. Add remaining oil and flour and make a roux in the same pot. Add vegetables and okra to the roux and cook for 5 minutes or until vegetables are tender. Add warm water and simmer for 1 hour. Add shrimp, seasoned with Tony's Creole Seasoning, and cook 30 minutes. Serve over steamed rice in a soup bowl and garnish with green onion and a sprinkling of filé. Yields 10 servings.

TONY'S SHRIMP STEW

1 pound shrimp, peeled
Tony's Creole Seasoning
4 tablespoons margarine
3 tablespoons all-purpose flour
1 onion, chopped

1 bell pepper, chopped
2 ribs celery, chopped
1 clove garlic, minced
1 tablespoon chopped
  green onions

Season shrimp with Tony's Creole Seasoning and refrigerate. Make a roux with margarine and flour in an aluminum Dutch oven. When chocolate colored, remove from heat and add all vegetables, except green onions. Stir mixture until it stops sizzling; add shrimp, and enough warm water to cover all ingredients. Return to heat and simmer for 30 minutes. Serve over steamed rice and garnish with green onions. Yields 4 servings.

You may substitute crawfish, crab meat, oysters, clams, or fish fillets.

CHICKEN AND OKRA GUMBO

1 (6 lb.) hen, cut up	2 ribs celery, chopped
Tony's Creole Seasoning	4 cloves garlic, minced
4 tablespoons oil	1 bell pepper, chopped
2 cups chopped fresh okra	3 quarts warm water
4 tablespoons margarine	2 tablespoons chopped green
4 tablespoons all-purpose flour	onions
1 onion, chopped	Filé

Season chicken with Tony's Creole Seasoning. In a large Dutch oven, fry chicken in 2 tablespoons oil until brown. Remove and set aside. Add 2 more tablespoons oil and fry chopped okra for 10 minutes, stirring constantly to keep from burning. In a separate pot, make a dark roux with the margarine and flour; add to okra. Add chicken, onion, celery, bell pepper, garlic, and water. Bring to a boil, then simmer for 2 hours or until chicken is tender. Skim off excess fat. Serve in soup bowls with steamed rice. Garnish with green onions and a sprinkling of filé. Yields 10 servings.

TONY'S OLD-FASHIONED CHICKEN STEW

Mushrooms can be added for a delicious variation.

1 (6 lb.) hen, cut up	4 cups warm water
1 tablespoon shortening	Tony's Creole Seasoning
2 tablespoons all-purpose flour	1/4 cup chopped green onions
3 onions, finely chopped	and parsley

In a Dutch oven, brown chicken in shortening; remove from pot. Place flour in pot and stir until brown. Add onions and cook until tender. Add chicken and water. Season with Tony's Creole Seasoning. Simmer until tender (about 1 hour). During the last 5 minutes of cooking, add green onions and parsley. Stir occasionally as stew thickens to prevent burning. Serve over steamed rice. Yields 6 servings.

CHICKEN FRICASSÉE

1 (6 lb.) hen or rooster, cut up
Tony's Creole Seasoning
4 tablespoons margarine
³/₄ cup milk
½ cup all-purpose flour

1 onion, finely chopped
2 ribs celery, chopped
1 bell pepper, chopped
3 cloves garlic, finely chopped
½ cup chopped green onions

Season chicken with Tony's Creole Seasoning. Melt margarine in
a Dutch oven. Dip chicken in milk, dredge in flour, and fry in
margarine until brown. Remove chicken. Sauté onion, celery, bell
pepper, and garlic in pot until tender. Add chicken and enough
water to cover. Cook slowly for 1 hour, or until chicken is tender.
At this point, add dumplings (recipe follows). Serve over steamed
rice and garnish with green onions. Yields 8 servings.

Dumplings

2 cups all-purpose flour
2 teaspoons baking powder

½ teaspoon salt
1 cup milk

In a bowl, sift together flour, baking powder, and salt. Add milk
slowly, stirring until batter is smooth. Drop by tablespoonful into
fricassée and bring to a rapid boil for 3 to 4 minutes. Lower heat
and continue to simmer another 10 minutes. Yields 18 dumplings.

*Hard to beat!
In fact, it's even
better reheated
the next day.*

TONY'S CHICKEN AND SAUSAGE JAMBALAYA

1 (3 lb.) fryer, cut up
Tony's Creole Seasoning
4 tablespoons margarine
4 onions, chopped
4 cloves garlic, minced

2 ribs celery, chopped
1 bell pepper, chopped
½ pound smoked pork sausage
3 cups uncooked rice
6 cups water

Season chicken generously with Tony's Creole Seasoning. Add margarine to a 5 quart Dutch oven and fry chicken until brown. Remove chicken from pot and add all vegetables. Sauté for 10 minutes. Add sausage and rice and cook for 10 minutes, mixing thoroughly. Return chicken to pot; add water and stir. Cover and simmer about 30 minutes or until rice is fully cooked. Yields 8 servings.

ISABELL'S CREOLE PORK ROAST

1 (5 lb.) pork roast
Tony's Creole Seasoning

1 cup basic vegetable mixture
(pg. 25)

Make 10 slits in roast. Add 1 tablespoon of Tony's Creole Seasoning to vegetable mixture; stuff mixture into slits equally. Rub seasoning all over roast.

Place roast in Dutch oven. Cook in a 350° oven until roast is brown. Cover, reduce heat to 300° and cook for 3 hours or until roast is tender. You may thicken the gravy with a mixture of water and flour. Skim off excess fat. Yields 10 servings.

LOUISIANA
MEAT LOAF

1 cup bread crumbs
½ cup red wine
1 pound ground beef
½ pound lean pork
3 tablespoons chopped onions

3 tablespoons finely chopped
  celery leaves
3 tablespoons minced parsley
Tony's Creole Seasoning

In a large bowl, moisten bread crumbs thoroughly with red wine. Add all other ingredients to bread mixture. Mold into a loaf (kneading with fingers is best). Place in a greased loaf pan and cover with the following sauce. Bake in a 325° oven for 1 hour and 15 minutes, basting frequently. Do not allow to dry out. Add beef broth when needed. Remove from oven, turn onto platter and slice. Yields 8 servings.

Sauce

1 cup catsup
¼ cup wine vinegar
2 tablespoons chili powder

Tony's Creole Seasoning
¼ teaspoon hot pepper sauce

In a bowl, mix above ingredients thoroughly and pour over meat loaf.

CAJUN ROLLED STEAK

1 large round steak
Tony's Creole Seasoning
1 onion, sliced
1 bell pepper, sliced

3 ribs celery, chopped
String or toothpicks
1 tablespoon oil

Season round steak with Tony's Creole Seasoning. Spread onion, bell pepper, and celery evenly on steak. Roll up jelly roll style and tie with string or secure with toothpicks. Place in a skillet with oil. Cook on medium heat until brown, adding a little water while cooking. Steak will make its own gravy. Cover and cook for 45 minutes or until tender. Adjust seasoning. Slice and serve over steamed rice. Yields 6 servings.

FRENCH BREAD

1 (½ oz.) packet yeast
2 cups warm water

1½ teaspoons salt
5 cups all-purpose flour

In a measuring cup, dissolve yeast in ¼ cup warm water. In a large bowl, add salt, 1¾ cups lukewarm water; stir in softened yeast. Slowly stir in flour. Turn onto floured board and knead 10 minutes until dough becomes smooth and elastic. Place dough in large, greased bowl and cover with waxed paper.

Allow dough to double in size, which takes about 2 hours. Remove and turn onto floured board and knead lightly.

Divide and shape dough into 2 long loaves. Cover and let rise on a greased baking sheet in a warm place until dough doubles in size. When half risen, cut diagonal slits a few times across the top. When fully risen, brush surface with milk and bake in a 400° oven for 50 minutes until golden. Yields 2 loaves.

TONY'S CABBAGE CASSEROLE

1 medium head cabbage
4 tablespoons margarine
1 pound lean ground meat
1 medium onion, chopped
2 cloves garlic, minced
Tony's Creole Seasoning

1 (10 ¾ oz.) can cream of
 mushroom soup
¼ cup chopped green onions
1 cup steamed rice
¼ cup bread crumbs

Cut cabbage in small chunks and in a medium pot, boil in salted water until tender, but still green. Drain and reserve the liquid. Melt margarine in a deep skillet and fry ground meat with onions and garlic until brown. Add Tony's Creole Seasoning. In a large bowl, mix cabbage with meat, adding mushroom soup, green onions, and rice.

Pour mixture into greased, flat baking dish. Top with bread crumbs. If you think the casserole is too dry, add some of the water from the boiled cabbage. Bake at 300° for 20 to 30 minutes. Yields 6 servings.

ZUCCHINI BREAD

3 eggs
1½ cups sugar
1 cup oil
3 teaspoons vanilla extract
3 cups all-purpose flour
3 teaspoons cinnamon

½ teaspoon baking powder
1 teaspoon salt
1½ teaspoons baking soda
2 cups diced, uncooked,
 unpeeled, zucchini
1 cup chopped nuts

In a large bowl, beat eggs until lemon colored; add sugar. Beat until fluffy. Beat in oil and vanilla. In a separate bowl, sift dry ingredients together. Add dry ingredients to egg mixture, and mix well. Add zucchini and nuts. Spoon into greased and floured loaf pans (8 ½ x 4 ½ x 2 ½ inch). Bake in a 350° oven for 1 hour. Yields 2 loaves.

41

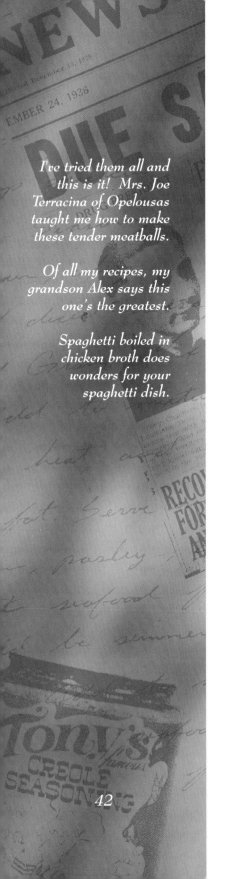

TONY'S MEAT BALLS AND SPAGHETTI

½ pound lean ground pork
½ pound lean ground beef
½ cup crushed crackers
1 tablespoon chopped parsley
½ cup chopped green onions

¼ cup grated Romano cheese
Tony's Creole Seasoning
1 cup milk
3 eggs, well beaten
1 cup olive oil

To make meat balls, in a large bowl, combine all ingredients, except milk and oil. Add enough milk to make a soft mixture. Wet hands with water and roll into 16 very soft meat balls (add milk to mixture if not soft enough). The trick to tender meatballs is to fill them with air rather than compacting them into a ball. Place meatball in hand cupped upward and gently toss the ball upward a few times to fill with air. Fry in oil in a heavy Dutch oven until brown. Remove from pot and set aside.

Sauce

1 onion, chopped
2 cloves garlic, minced
½ bell pepper, chopped
2 (6 oz.) cans tomato paste
1 tablespoon sugar

1 fresh basil leaf
10 or more anise seeds to taste
1 quart water
Tony's Creole Seasoning

To the same Dutch oven add onion, garlic, and bell pepper. Sauté until tender. Add tomato paste; cook for 10 minutes. Add sugar, basil, anise and water. Simmer for 1 hour. Add meat balls and cook slowly for an additional hour. Adjust seasoning. Skim off excess fat. Pour over spaghetti and serve. Yields 8 servings.

HOMEMADE PEACH
ICE CREAM

³/₄ cup sugar

1 tablespoon all-purpose flour

¹/₄ teaspoon salt

2 egg yolks

1 cup milk

3 cups light cream

2 cups sliced, sweetened
  peaches

¹/₄ teaspoon almond extract

Gallon size ice cream freezer

Ice

1 box freezer salt

In a double boiler, combine sugar, flour, and salt. In a small bowl, beat egg yolks slightly; add milk and mix well. Stir into sugar mixture. Cook over hot water, stirring constantly, until thickened. Pour into a large bowl; let cool. Add cream, peaches, and extract.

Place dasher in freezer can; add ice cream mixture. Cover and adjust crank. Pack 8 parts ice to 1 part freezer salt around can. Turn dasher slowly until ice partially melts, forming a brine. After 5 to 10 minutes, increase speed and turn constantly until turning becomes difficult.

Remove ice from around top of can; take off lid and remove dasher. Plug opening in lid and replace lid. Drain off brine. Pack 4 parts ice to 1 part salt around freezer can. Cover and let stand 3 or 4 hours to ripen. Yields 1¹/₃ quarts.

We used to make this when I was a kid. Since I turned the crank, I got to lick the dasher.

*"Some of the best pork recipes
still used by Cajuns today originated from
the shared activity called the boucherie."*

OUTDOOR COOKING

NOTHING BUT THE SQUEAL

Some of the best pork recipes still used by Cajuns today originated from the shared activity called the boucherie, which was like a multi-family party.

Everyone used to raise their own animals. One hog would yield more meat than one family could eat before it spoiled, so each family took turns butchering one and sharing it with everyone.

The boucherie was a long day of hard work. It began with the men slaying the hog, while the women prepared for the sausage and boudin making. A big black iron pot sat on an open fire, awaiting the hog's cleaned skin for making cracklins.

It is often said that the only part of the poor hog that was left over was the squeal. We saved his heart and liver for bouilli. His head was used to make hog's head cheese. Of course, there were nice chops and ham to share. Women ground other meaty parts and either made pork sausage for smoking or boudin blanc. Even the creature's feet were saved for pickling!

Despite the hard work, the boucherie was a pretty fun day. The women would save the choice meat of the backbone to make reintier, or backbone stew, for the whole group to enjoy. Sometimes a couple of the older men brought along an accordion and a little iron triangle and entertained the group with an hour or so of Cajun melodies.

The day could not pass without one of the naive young boys being "initiated" by the balloon trick. I remember my turn. During the butchering process, the men saved the pig's balloon and lured me to see if I wanted it. I was delighted and ran over with it to show off to the other kids. The older boys started laughing. I wondered why because I thought I was holding a prize. One gal, seeing my puzzled look, walked over and whispered in my ear. My face instantly turned red as my hands opened and dumped my prize on the ground.

I had been holding the hog's bladder!

OUTDOOR COOKING
Contents

GRATONS
Cracklings

3 pounds fresh pork skins with
  about ¹/₂ inch fat on skin
2 tablespoons baking soda

Water
Salt

Cut pork skins in 1 inch squares. Place in a heavy pot. Start cooking on medium heat. When the cracklings get hot, add a little water and soda so the cracklings do not stick. Stir constantly; repeat water process to keep them from sticking. Stop adding water when the cracklings begin to fry in about 1 inch of their own fat. Stir often until cracklings are crispy and brown. Drain on absorbent paper and salt generously. Great! Yields 15 servings.

HOG'S HEAD
CHEESE

1 hog head, cleaned, cut into 4
4 hog feet, cleaned
3 pounds lean pork
4 cloves garlic, minced
¹/₂ bell pepper, chopped
1 cup chopped onions

Tony's Creole Seasoning
1 (1 oz.) package plain gelatin
1 cup chopped green onions
  and parsley
¹/₂ sweet red pepper, or
  pimiento, chopped

Put head, feet, pork, garlic, bell pepper, and onions in a large pot. Cover with water and boil until meat falls from bones. Remove meat and chop or grind, discard bones. Cook remaining broth down to about 2 quarts. Strain; place meat and broth in saucepan. Season generously with Tony's Creole Seasoning. Add gelatin softened in water. Cook for 15 minutes. Add green onions, parsley, and sweet red pepper. Pour into several loaf pans to mold. Place in refrigerator overnight to set. Yields 4 loaves.

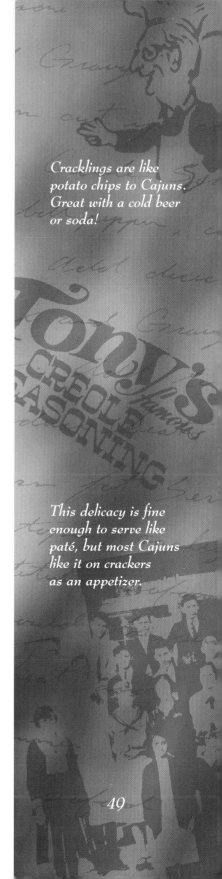

Cracklings are like potato chips to Cajuns. Great with a cold beer or soda!

This delicacy is fine enough to serve like paté, but most Cajuns like it on crackers as an appetizer.

49

JOHNSON'S BOUDIN BLANC

White Boudin

1 (4 lb.) Boston butt roast	Steamed rice (use 2 cups for
1 pound pork liver	each cup finished mixture)
3 cups basic vegetable mixture	Tony's Creole Seasoning
(pg. 25)	1 package pork casings
1 cup chopped green onions	(from your local packing house)
½ cup chopped parsley	

Put all meat through a meat grinder. In a large pot, cover meat with water; bring to a boil and simmer for 1 to 2 hours until cooked. Pour off excess liquid and reserve. In a large mixing bowl, combine meat with basic vegetable mixture, green onions and parsley; add rice. Mix well and season generously with Tony's Creole Seasoning. If too dry, add reserved liquid. Fill casings using a sausage stuffing machine and tie ends. Place in gently boiling water for 30 minutes.
Yields 12 servings.

BARBECUED ONIONS

1 Bermuda onion	1 tablespoon chili powder
2 tablespoons barbecue sauce	Tony's Creole Seasoning
4 tablespoons all-purpose flour	1 tablespoon margarine

Peel onion. Remove ends. Cut onion into ¼ inch thick slices. Separate onion slices into rings. Spread completely with barbecue sauce; dust with flour on both sides and sprinkle chili powder and Tony's Creole Seasoning over both sides. Place rings on greased flat baking sheet; brush lightly with melted margarine: place in broiler until golden brown, turning only once. Yields 2 servings.

TONY'S CREOLE
BARBECUE SAUCE

So good you can eat it on bread!

4 cups oil
1 pod garlic, minced
6 ribs celery, chopped
2 pounds onions, chopped

5 bell peppers, chopped
2 cups water
Tony's Creole Seasoning

In a large pot combine all vegetables. Season with Tony's Creole Seasoning and cook for 2 hours, then add to the pot:

1 pound margarine
1 (6 oz.) jar yellow mustard
1 (14 oz.) bottle chili sauce
Juice from 1 lemon

2 tablespoons Worcestershire
    sauce
1 (3 oz.) bottle hot pepper sauce
4 cups water

Cook until well blended. Use the oil on top for basting and serve the cooked vegetables as a side dish. Yields about 2 quarts.

GRILLED
PARMESAN CORN

12 half ears of corn
1/4 cup melted margarine
2 tablespoons Parmesan cheese

1 tablespoon parsley flakes
Tony's Creole Seasoning
Foil

In a soup bowl, stir cheese, parsley, and seasoning into margarine. Roll each ear of corn in the mixture to coat. Wrap each ear in foil and place on grill about 3 to 4 minutes before other foods are ready. Turn once after 2 minutes. Remove promptly and leave wrapped until ready to serve. Yields 12 servings.

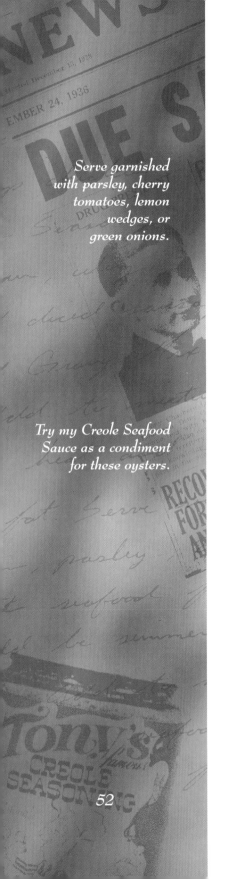

Serve garnished with parsley, cherry tomatoes, lemon wedges, or green onions.

Try my Creole Seafood Sauce as a condiment for these oysters.

GRILLED CATFISH FILLETS

Italian dressing
Mustard
Worcestershire sauce

2 (7 oz.) catfish fillets
Tony's Creole Seasoning

In a small bowl, mix Italian dressing, mustard, and Worcestershire sauce. Rub on fillets. Sprinkle Tony's Creole Seasoning on fillets. Allow to marinate 1 hour in refrigerator. Use charcoal grill. Grill fillets 3 minutes on each side. Yields 2 servings.

GRILLED OYSTERS

For this recipe, oysters are bought by the sackful in the shells, singles or in clusters. An outdoor fireplace or grill can be used. Build a hot fire, and when the grill becomes hot, cover it with oysters. Turn until the shells start to open. They are then ready to eat. Yields 6 oysters per serving.

BOILED CRAWFISH

10 pounds crawfish   *1 cup Tony's Crawfish and*
Crab Boil

Place crawfish in the metal basket of a deep boiling pot (20 gallon or larger). Place the basket of crawfish in the pot and fill with enough water to cover crawfish. Remove the basket of crawfish and set aside.

Add seasoning to water and bring to a boil. Place basket of crawfish in boiling water. When water returns to a boil, allow the crawfish to boil for 5 minutes. When boiling time is complete, remove from heat, cover and allow the crawfish to soak for 15 minutes. Remove basket from the water and serve. Yields 2 servings.

This method can also be used for the following foods:

Crabs (24–30 medium)   1 lb. seasoning, 10 minutes boiling, 15 minutes soaking.

Shrimp (20 lb. medium)   1 lb. seasoning, 1 minute boiling, 15 minutes soaking.

Corn on the Cob (30 halves)   1 lb. seasoning, 20 minutes boiling, no soaking.

Potatoes (10 lb.)   1 lb. seasoning, 30 minutes boiling, no soaking.

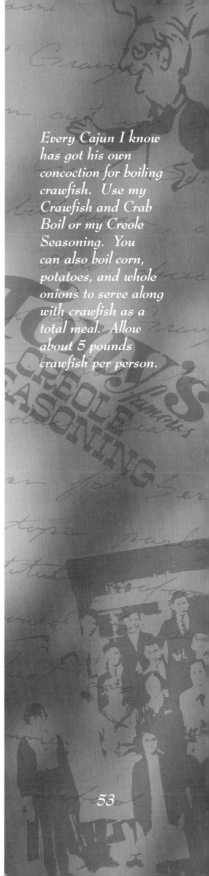

Every Cajun I know has got his own concoction for boiling crawfish. Use my Crawfish and Crab Boil or my Creole Seasoning. You can also boil corn, potatoes, and whole onions to serve along with crawfish as a total meal. Allow about 5 pounds crawfish per person.

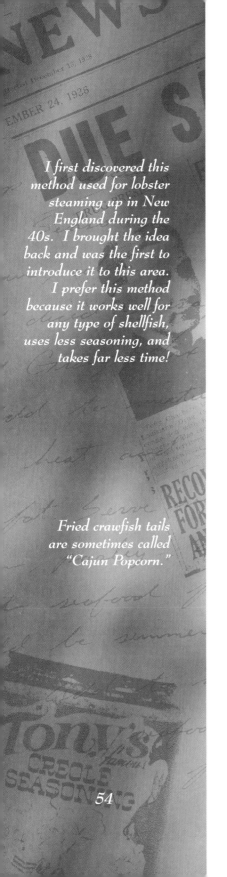

54

TONY'S
STEAMED CRAWFISH

1 tablespoon oil   *Tony's Crawfish and Crab Boil*
10 pounds crawfish   *or Tony's Creole Seasoning*

Pour about 3 inches of water into a large pot. Add oil. Use no seasoning. When water comes to a boil, place crawfish in the water and cover. When steam begins to escape, begin timing: 5 minutes for crawfish, 2 minutes for shrimp, 10 minutes for crabs. Have a styrofoam chest ready. Remove the boiled crawfish (or other seafood) from the water and place a layer of them in the chest. Shake on a generous layer of seasoning. Continue to layer crawfish then seasoning until chest is full. Cover tightly and let stand for 20 to 30 minutes to steam. Serve immediately. Yields 2 servings.

TONY'S FRIED
CRAWFISH TAILS

2 eggs   *1 pound peeled crawfish tails*
1 (5 oz.) can evaporated milk   *Tony's Creole Seasoning*
1 tablespoon baking powder   *1 cup all-purpose flour*
2 tablespoons vinegar   *Oil for frying*

In a large bowl, mix eggs, milk, baking powder, and vinegar. Season crawfish tails with Tony's Creole Seasoning and marinate in mixture at least 1 hour. Remove, dip each crawfish tail in flour and deep fry in 380° oil until golden brown. Yields 4 servings.

FRIED
SOFT SHELL CRABS

6 soft shell crabs
1 cup milk
1 egg

Tony's Creole Seasoning
1 cup all-purpose flour
Oil for frying

Garnish with lemon slices and chopped parsley and serve with tartar sauce.

Clean crabs and wash thoroughly in cold water and dry on absorbent paper.

In a large bowl, mix milk and egg; season with Tony's Creole Seasoning. Soak crabs in this mixture for 1 hour. Roll in flour and deep fry in 375° oil until golden brown. Yields 6 servings.

BRICE PALMER'S
FRIED ALLIGATOR

3 pounds boneless alligator
  meat, cut in 1 inch cubes
3 cups milk
1 cup mustard

Tony's Creole Seasoning
4 cups pancake mix
Oil for frying

In a large bowl, soak meat in milk in the refrigerator for 2 to 3 hours. Drain milk and season meat in the same bowl with Tony's Creole Seasoning. Add mustard and mix well. Place pancake mix in a shaking bag. Drop meat cubes in shaking bag and coat well. Deep fry at 375° for 5 to 6 minutes or until golden brown. Serve hot with French fries and seafood sauce. Yields 8 servings.

55

FRENCH-FRIED SWEET POTATOES

4 sweet potatoes   Oil for frying
$\frac{1}{4}$ cup sugar or cinnamon sugar

Peel sweet potatoes and cut into $\frac{1}{2}$ to $\frac{3}{4}$ inch strips. In a bowl, soak the potatoes in cold, salted water for 10 minutes; drain and dry between towels. Deep fry in 365° oil for 3 to 5 minutes or until golden brown. Drain on absorbent paper and sprinkle lightly with sugar. Serve with pork chops, steaks, or ham. Yields 8 servings.

JIM BOWIE'S HUSH PUPPIES

2 cups corn meal   Tony's Creole Seasoning
1 cup all-purpose flour   2 tablespoons baking powder
2 tablespoons minced onions   Milk
1 egg   Oil for frying
2 tablespoons bacon drippings

In a bowl, mix all ingredients with just enough milk to make a thick mixture. Wet hands and roll mixture into $1\frac{1}{2}$ inch balls. Deep fry in 375° oil until golden brown. Drain on absorbent paper. Yields 24 hush puppies.

CARROT
BEIGNETS

5 pounds carrots
4 eggs
3 tablespoons vanilla extract
6 cups sugar

1 teaspoon cinnamon
7 cups self-rising flour
Oil for frying

Cut the carrots into small chunks. In a pot, boil the carrots until they are tender. Mash the carrots in a large bowl. Add eggs, vanilla, sugar, and cinnamon; beat well. Add flour and blend until a soft dough forms. Add a little more flour if necessary. Drop by tablespoonful into hot oil set at a consistent 350°. Fry until golden on both sides. Yields 4 to 5 dozen beignets.

TONY'S
DEEP-FRIED TURKEY

1 (approximately 14 lb.) turkey

Mix the following ingredients in a blender 2 days before cooking. Pour into a jar and refrigerate.

1 tablespoon Worcestershire sauce
2 tablespoons Creole mustard
3 (2 oz.) bottles garlic juice
3 (2 oz.) bottles onion juice

1 (3 oz.) bottle hot pepper sauce
1/4 cup Tony's Creole Seasoning
8 ounces water

Inject turkey with a syringe using the blended mixture. Rub turkey with additional mustard and season generously with Tony's Creole Seasoning. When ready to cook, heat 5 gallons of peanut oil to 350°; submerge turkey and let fry for 4 minutes per pound of turkey. Yields 15 servings.

My friends, Ben Bourque and Obey Roy, are two outstanding camp cooks in Abbeville. From crawfish boil to cochon de lait, they've done it all and then some! Their carrot beignets go well with fried fish. I like them with gumbo.

You can keep this marinade in the refrigerator for months. Use at Thanksgiving, then again at Christmas.

THE CAJUN MICROWAVE

No one can ever accuse a Cajun of being uninventive. Cajuns are about the most resourceful people on earth. Leave it to the Cajuns to develop another fun, unique way to cook outdoors. That's how the Cajun Microwave came about.

The Cajun Microwave is a wooden charcoal-heated box used for cooking meats outdoors. The one I've got is made of thick plywood, one-half inch brick insulation and 26-gauge metal. The inside of the box is lined with the metal. The top of the box is constructed with a metal tray "hot box" in its center to hold the hot charcoal. The hot charcoal radiates heat throughout the box and cooks the meat inside.

What can you cook in the Cajun Microwave? I've used mine for a venison hindquarter, for an alligator roast or tail, and for lamb with a medley of vegetables. Most folks love it for the ultimate Cajun cookout, the "cochon de lait."

Roasting the "milk pig" or suckling pig is by far the most popular Cajun outdoor cooking event. We usually hold the cochon de lait to celebrate some important event or holiday, like Easter, a family reunion, New Year's Day, or a wedding rehearsal dinner. Since the pig generally takes about four hours to cook, sitting around the Cajun Microwave and having a few cool ones gives everyone a place to gather outdoors. Throw in an accordion and you've got one hell of a party!

One word of caution about the Cajun Microwave: it tends to release the most heavenly aroma as your meat cooks. Your neighbors and long-lost cousins will come out of the woodwork.

Be prepared with extra for uninvited guests!

PORK BACKBONE STEW

4 tablespoons margarine
4 tablespoons all-purpose flour
1 onion, chopped
1/2 bell pepper, chopped
2 ribs celery, chopped

2 cloves garlic, minced
4 pounds pork backbone pieces
Tony's Creole Seasoning
4 cups water

In a Dutch oven, make a dark roux with flour and margarine. Add vegetables and sauté for 1 or 2 minutes. Add pork backbone pieces, Tony's Creole Seasoning, and enough water to cover. Bring to a boil; simmer about 2 hours or until tender. If too thick, add water. Skim excess fat. Serve over steamed rice. Yields 8 servings.

HARRY'S PORK RIB JAMBALAYA

2 pounds pork ribs
1 tablespoon oil
1 onion, chopped
1 bell pepper, chopped
1 rib celery, chopped

4 cups water
2 cups rice
1/2 cup chopped green onions
Tony's Creole Seasoning
Parsley, finely chopped

In a Dutch oven, cook pork ribs in oil on medium heat, adding a little water at a time until brown. Add onions, bell pepper, and celery; cook for 5 minutes. Add water; bring to a boil. Reduce heat and simmer for 45 minutes. Add rice, green onions, and Tony's Creole Seasoning. Cook for 30 minutes. Add parsley during the last 5 minutes of cooking. Yields 8 servings.

About 6 medium-size turnips added to the stew is delicious.

Be sure to select meaty pork ribs for this dish.

59

Some cooks prefer to continue the cooking in a heavy pot on top of the stove instead of in the oven; however, great care must be taken not to let it burn at the bottom.

Great in the Cajun Microwave, too.

DIRTY RICE

1 pound chicken giblets
1 pound ground beef
1 cup chopped onions
½ cup chopped bell pepper
½ cup chopped celery with
  leaves

¼ cup chopped parsley
Juice of 2 crushed garlic cloves
Tony's Creole Seasoning
¼ cup chopped green onions
Pinch thyme and basil
2 cups rice

In a pot, boil giblets in salt water until tender; reserve liquid. In a Dutch oven, sauté meats until brown. Drain off excess fat, add remaining ingredients, and continue to cook a few minutes. In a separate pot, cook rice in 4 cups of giblet liquid for 18 minutes. Drain rice and mix thoroughly into the meat mixture. Spoon into a greased casserole and bake at 300° for 20 to 30 minutes or until dry. Yields 10 servings.

LIME MARINATED SPARERIBS

¾ cup lime juice
½ cup oil
3 tablespoons brown sugar
½ teaspoon coriander

½ teaspoon ginger
Tony's Creole Seasoning
1 (4 lb.) strip of spareribs
1 lime cut in wedges

In a bowl, combine all ingredients, except spareribs. Place spareribs in a shallow baking dish and cover with marinade mixture. Cover and refrigerate overnight. Drain and reserve marinade. Place spareribs, rib side up, on rack in a roasting pan and cover tightly. Bake at 350° for 30 minutes. Uncover, turn over and brush with reserved marinade. Continue to bake for 1½ hours, brushing with reserved marinade every 30 minutes. Remove from oven and serve. Garnish with lime wedges. Yields 4 servings.

TONY'S
BLACKENED FILLETS

6 (10 oz.) fish fillets,
3 sticks butter, melted

Tony's Blackening Seasoning

Heat a large cast–iron skillet over very high heat until it is beyond the smoking stage (at least 10 minutes). Do this in a well–ventilated area, preferably outdoors.

Meanwhile, dip each fillet in the melted butter so that both sides are well coated. Sprinkle Tony's Blackening Seasoning generously and evenly on both sides of the fillets. Place fillets in the hot skillet and pour 1 teaspoon melted butter on top of each (watch carefully as butter may flame). Cook, uncovered, over the same heat until the underside looks charred (about 2 minutes). Turn the fish over and pour 1 teaspoon butter on top. Cook until fish is done. Repeat with remaining fillets; serve while piping hot. Yields 6 servings.

SKEWERED
OYSTERS

24 oysters, shucked
Lemon juice

Tony's Creole Seasoning
24 strips bacon

Drain oysters; discard liquor. Season with lemon juice and Tony's Creole Seasoning. Wrap each oyster in a strip of bacon and thread on skewer, leaving some space between wrapped oysters. Broil under moderate heat, turning frequently, for 15 minutes or until bacon is crisp and thoroughly cooked (or rest skewers on rim of baking pan and bake in a 425° oven for 15 minutes). Yields 6 servings.

Almost any firm fleshed fish will work for blackening. I recommend redfish, snapper or salmon. My Blackening Seasoning is also great for grilling shrimp and steaks.

Shrimp also work well for this recipe.

61

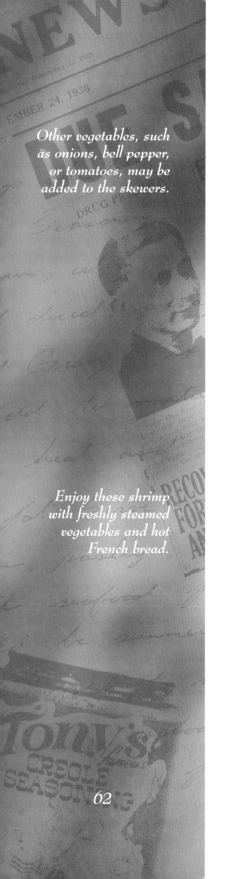

Other vegetables, such as onions, bell pepper, or tomatoes, may be added to the skewers.

Enjoy these shrimp with freshly steamed vegetables and hot French bread.

SHRIMP KABOBS

1½ pounds shrimp
4 slices bacon, cut in squares
Fresh mushrooms

3 tablespoons margarine
Tony's Creole Seasoning

Peel shrimp and devein. Wash shrimp and drain on absorbent paper. Using long skewers, alternate shrimp, squares of bacon, and mushrooms until the skewers are filled. In a small saucepan, melt margarine and add Tony's Creole Seasoning. Brush kabobs with seasoned margarine and place on a preheated, greased broiler pan about 3 inches from the source of heat. Broil 3 minutes, then turn and brush with margarine. Broil 1 to 1½ minutes longer. Yields 6 servings.

BROILED SHRIMP WITH BACON

4 tablespoons sherry
4 tablespoons soy sauce
1½ finely chopped slices
  fresh ginger
¼ teaspoon garlic

2 tablespoons honey
2 tablespoons corn starch
1 pound medium to large shrimp
Bacon
Toothpicks

In a small saucepan, prepare a sauce by combining sherry, soy sauce, ginger, garlic, and honey. Heat gently to dissolve the honey. In a measuring cup, combine several tablespoonfuls of the liquid with corn starch and make a thin paste. Pour this back into the sauce and cook over low heat until it is thick, stirring constantly. Set aside.

Peel shrimp; wrap each with a half strip of bacon and secure with a toothpick. Place the shrimp in a shallow casserole. Preheat oven to broil, and broil shrimp for 9 minutes or until shrimp are pink and bacon is crispy. Serve the shrimp and sauce hot. The shrimp are dipped into the sauce to eat. Yields 4 servings.

GRILLED TROUT
WITH DILL SAUCE

4 (8 oz.) speckled trout fillets
1 cup white wine
$\frac{1}{4}$ cup olive oil
$\frac{1}{4}$ cup Creole mustard
Tony's Creole Seasoning

1 cup sour cream
1 cup mayonnaise
2 tablespoons dill
1 teaspoon lemon juice

Rinse fillets and pat dry. Set aside. In a bowl, combine the next 4 ingredients and blend well. Lay fillets in an oblong dish and cover with wine marinade. Refrigerate for 2 to 4 hours.

In another bowl, combine the next 5 ingredients to create the Dill Sauce. Refrigerate until fillets are ready to serve.

When the grill is ready, spray the rack with cooking spray. Place fillets on rack. Cook the fillets about 8 minutes.

Place each fillet on a dinner plate. Ladle Dill Sauce over fillets and serve immediately. Yields 4 fillets.

"The sky became black,
filled with a canopy of millions of flapping, calling birds.
I had never seen so many ducks in my life!"

CAMP COOKING

DUCK HUNTING IN GUEYDAN

In the 1940s, I took to the road for my business, Louisiana Drug Company. As a drummer, I had the opportunity to meet many colorful characters in many unique corners of the Gulf Coast. One such place was Wright, Louisiana.

Wright was once a railroad stop between Kaplan and Gueydan in Vermilion Parish. At the station was the Wright Warehouse, a place where locals could purchase a wide array of goods. On a sales call there, I met Ulysse Saltzman of Gueydan, who invited me to accompany him on a hunting trip with his son-in-law, Otis Abshire, and friend, Tee Blanc Adams. I was thrilled to be invited on this trip after hearing that Otis was a world champion duck caller!

It was cold and nasty that morning, the perfect duck hunting weather. I brought along my friend Dr. Zoder that day, so there were five of us in Tee Blanc's pirogue, plus his big black Lab.

On our trek into the marsh, the Lab jumped out of the pirogue twice to kill a raccoon. Blanc was delighted because he sold the hides.

As we approached the blind, there was suddenly the most deafening sound, a thundering like that of a freight train. The sky became black, filled with a canopy of millions of flapping, calling birds. I had never seen so many ducks in my life!

Apparently we had spooked them. We paddled on and in a few minutes reached the blind. We settled in and had our eyes peeled to sight the first group.

"Tony," Otis said in his flat Cajun accent, "mais, you see dat li'l teal dere? I can make 'im land right here," and he pointed down to the water right outside the blind.

I looked up at the tiny flapping dot so far off in the sky and listened to Otis call for him. The little bird responded immediately. I watched it circle, come in for a landing and then felt my mouth hang open in amazement. The little teal swam up so close to the blind that I could've reached out and hit him with a stick. I had witnessed the first of a morning full of great calls by my new friend, the duck-calling champion.

He called in group after group that morning and we picked 'em off one after the other. In no time we had quite a collection. I was having so much fun there that I don't remember shivering, not even once....

We shot about 35 mallards that morning. We also took down seven pretty ringnecks. As we loaded up for the trip back, I suddenly realized what a haul we had for that pirogue: seven geese which totaled about eighty pounds, 35 ducks, 5 men, all our gear, 2 coons, and one big, wet Lab. As we paddled through the marsh, I looked nervously from side to side. The water came within an inch of spilling into the pirogue. I tapped Otis on the shoulder and pointed down at the water.

"Aw, don't be afraid, Tony," Otis reassured me. "The water's not but two feet deep!"

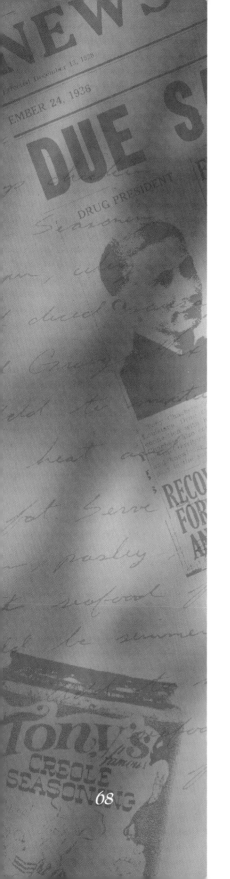

CAMP COOKING
Contents

BAKED TEAL WITH OYSTERS

6 teal, dressed
Tony's Creole Seasoning
1½ dozen fresh oysters
1 stick margarine, sliced
½ onion, finely chopped
Toothpicks or needle and thread
2 strips bacon, cut in thirds

1 (10 ½ oz.) can chicken broth
½ cup Burgundy wine
½ cup chopped green onions
  and parsley
1 (4 oz.) can mushrooms
2 tablespoons currant jelly
1 tablespoon all-purpose flour

Season teal inside and out with Tony's Creole Seasoning. Stuff 3 oysters in each duck with a slice of margarine and a teaspoonful of onion. Close with toothpicks or thread.

Melt remaining margarine in a large roaster. Place birds, breast side up, in roaster; add bacon on top. Cook uncovered until brown in 450° oven. Add broth and wine. Reduce oven to 300°; cover and cook about 1 hour. Turn over on breast and cook about 1 more hour or until ducks are tender. When tender enough to remove breast bone, remove birds from roaster. To pan drippings, add green onions, parsley, mushrooms, and jelly. Mix mushroom juice with flour and add to gravy. Cook for 5 minutes or until thickened. Serve over steamed rice. Yields 6 servings.

When we've been on duck hunts together, my son Doug insists on my Baked Teal. You can substitute mallard or pintail in this recipe.

69

WILD DUCKS A LA GEORGE

4 ducks, dressed	1 cup Burgundy wine
Tony's Creole Seasoning	2 (10 ½ oz.) cans chicken broth
4 onions, chopped	½ cup chopped green onions
4 ribs celery, chopped	½ cup chopped parsley
1 bell pepper, chopped	1 (8 oz.) can mushrooms
4 tablespoons oil	½ tablespoon all-purpose flour

Season ducks inside and out generously with Tony's Creole Seasoning. In a small bowl, mix the vegetables. Add equally to inside of each duck.

Pour oil in a large black iron pot. Brown ducks. Add wine, chicken broth, and enough water to cover ducks. Bring to a boil. Reduce heat; simmer until tender (about 3 to 4 hours). Remove ducks from pot. Add green onions, parsley, mushrooms, and mushroom juice thickened with a little flour. Cook 5 minutes. Add water if more gravy is needed. Yields 8 servings.

FRIED DOVES

10 doves	1 egg
Tony's Creole Seasoning	2 cups pancake flour
1 cup milk	Oil for frying

Clean doves, singe, split down the back and flatten. Season with Tony's Creole Seasoning. In a bowl, soak in mixture of milk and egg. When ready to fry, dip in pancake flour and deep fry in 375° oil. When doves float to the top, remove and drain on absorbent paper. The secret of tender doves is quick frying. Yields 5 servings.

SMOTHERED DOVES
ACADIENNE

8 tablespoons margarine
8 doves, cleaned
2 onions, chopped
2 ribs celery, chopped
1 bell pepper, chopped
4 cloves garlic, finely chopped
1 cup Burgundy wine

1 (4 oz.) can mushrooms
1 tablespoon all-purpose flour
2 tablespoons chopped green
  onions
1 tablespoon chopped parsley
Tony's Creole Seasoning
Currant jelly, optional

Melt margarine in Dutch oven; add doves and cook until brown, stirring constantly until they begin to stick to the bottom. Add onions, celery, bell pepper, and garlic. Cook until tender. Add wine; cover and simmer for 2 to 3 hours or until birds are tender. Doves are tough and need a long time to cook. Add cold water as needed.

When doves are tender, remove from pot and transfer to serving platter. Add mushrooms, a mixture of flour blended with the mushroom juice, green onions, and parsley. Season with Tony's Creole Seasoning. If you like a sweet gravy, add 2 tablespoons of currant jelly. Yields 8 servings.

My son Doug and I have made numerous trips to the Lake Guerrera area in Mexico to hunt white wing doves. A great camp cook himself, he loves my dove recipes, especially this one.

71

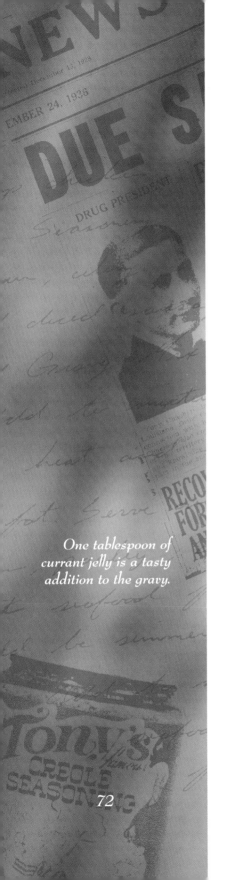

GRILLED QUAIL

16 quail, dressed
16 Jalapeño peppers
16 slices bacon
1 (8 oz.) bottle Italian salad
  dressing

$\frac{1}{2}$ cup Chablis
$\frac{1}{3}$ cup soy sauce
$\frac{1}{4}$ cup lemon juice
Tony's Creole Seasoning
Banana peppers, optional

Rinse quail thoroughly with water; pat dry. Place a Jalapeño pepper into body cavity of each quail. Wrap 1 bacon slice around each quail and secure with a toothpick. Place quail in a large shallow dish. In a bowl, combine Italian dressing and next 4 ingredients; pour over quail. Cover and marinate in refrigerator overnight.

Remove quail from dish, reserving marinade. Prepare charcoal fire in one end of grill; burn 15 to 20 minutes, or until flames disappear and coals are white. Grill quail, covered, on opposite end for 1 hour, turning once, and basting often with marinade. Garnish with banana peppers, if desired. Yields 8 servings.

TONY'S BAKED QUAIL

One tablespoon of currant jelly is a tasty addition to the gravy.

6 quail
4 tablespoons margarine
1 tablespoon chopped onions
1 tablespoon chopped celery
1 tablespoon chopped bell pepper

1 cup chicken broth
1 tablespoon Sherry wine
Tony's Creole Seasoning
1 (4 oz.) can mushrooms
1 tablespoon all-purpose flour

Season quail and sauté in margarine in a Dutch oven until brown. In a small bowl, mix onions, celery, and bell pepper. Remove birds from pot and stuff each cavity with 1 teaspoon of chopped vegetables. Return to pot and add broth, wine, and the remainder of the vegetable mixture. Season with Tony's Creole Seasoning. Cover, place in 300° oven and cook 1 hour or until tender. Place pot on stove top and remove quail, placing them on a serving dish. Add mushrooms and flour to the gravy and simmer for 5 minutes. Yields 6 servings.

72

SWAMP RABBIT

1 (3 lb.) rabbit, cut up
Tony's Creole Seasoning
1 cup all-purpose flour
4 tablespoons margarine
1 onion, chopped

1 bell pepper, chopped
2 ribs celery, chopped
4 cloves garlic, minced
1 (6 oz.) can tomato paste

Season rabbit well with Tony's Creole Seasoning. Dip in flour and fry in a Dutch oven in margarine until brown. Add onions, bell pepper, celery, and garlic; simmer until vegetables are tender. Add tomato paste and enough water to cook rabbit until tender and still have a nice, thick gravy. Serve over steamed rice. Yields 4 servings.

SMOTHERED
RABBIT STEW

2 rabbits, cut up
Tony's Creole Seasoning
1/4 cup oil
2 onions, chopped
1/2 bell pepper, chopped

2 ribs celery, chopped
1 teaspoon garlic powder
2 cups water
1 (10 3/4 oz.) can cream of
   mushroom soup

Season meat with Tony's Creole Seasoning. In a Dutch oven, brown meat in oil to barely cover the bottom of the pot. Remove meat from the pot. Add onions, bell pepper, celery, and garlic; cook until tender. Return meat to the pot and add water. Cook for 1 1/2 hours or until tender. Add cream of mushroom soup, blend well, and cook 15 minutes longer. Yields 6 servings.

For best results, use wild rabbits. Makes a fantastic gravy.

73

ROASTED RABBIT

1 rabbit	1 sprig parsley, chopped
½ cup ground pork	1 sprig thyme, crushed
½ cup ground beef	1 bay leaf, crushed
1 egg, beaten	4 cloves garlic, minced
1 cup bread crumbs	1 cup hot water
Tony's Creole Seasoning	1 cup milk
1 tablespoon all-purpose flour	4 tablespoons margarine,
1 onion, chopped	melted
1 carrot, chopped	½ cup white wine

Clean rabbit and soak in slightly salted water for 1 hour. Dry and
rub well with Tony's Creole Seasoning. In a bowl, prepare dressing
by mixing ground meats with egg; add bread crumbs and Tony's
Creole Seasoning to the mixture. Stuff rabbit with dressing mixture.
Close opening with toothpicks. Sift flour over top of rabbit and
place in roasting pan on a bed of onions, carrots, parsley, thyme, bay
leaf, and garlic. Moisten with hot water. Cover and roast in 300°
oven for 2 hours. Baste every 15 minutes with milk during the
first hour. Baste with melted margarine during the second hour of
cooking. Before serving, add wine to gravy and pour over rabbit.
Yields 4 servings.

ROUGHNECK
HOT ROLLS

1 cup warm water	¾ cup shortening
½ cup sugar	6 cups all-purpose flour
2 (¼ oz.) packages dry yeast	½ teaspoon salt

Put warm water in a large mixing bowl. Add sugar to warm water;
add yeast and let stand. Let yeast come to top of the water; add
shortening. Add flour and salt. Mix well. Place in greased mixing
bowl. Let dough rise to twice the original size. Roll dough out on
floured board to ¾ inch thickness. Cut rolls and place in greased
pan; let rise. Bake at 400° for 20 minutes or until golden brown.
Butter tops and serve. Yields 18 rolls.

TONY'S BISCUITS

5 cups self–rising flour
1 teaspoon baking soda
⅓ cup sugar

½ cup oil
2 (¼ oz.) packages yeast
2 cups buttermilk

In a large bowl, sift flour, soda, and sugar together. Add oil and blend. Dissolve yeast in ¼ cup warm water and add with buttermilk to mixture. Mix well. Place on floured cutting board, cut into biscuits, and place on greased baking sheets. Bake in 400° oven until brown. Yields 36 biscuits.

CAJUN SQUIRREL STEW
The one and only

4 squirrels
Tony's Creole Seasoning
4 tablespoons margarine
1 cup chopped onions
½ cup chopped bell pepper
4 cloves garlic, chopped
1 cup water

½ cup Burgundy wine
1 tablespoon all-purpose flour
1 (4 oz.) can mushrooms
1 tablespoon chopped
 green onions
1 tablespoon chopped parsley

Cut each squirrel into eight pieces, including the heads. Season with Tony's Creole Seasoning. Melt margarine in a Dutch oven and fry meat until browned all over and it starts to stick to the pot. Add onions, bell pepper, and garlic. When vegetables are tender, add water and wine; cover the pot and simmer for 1 hour or until tender.

Remove meat from the pot. Add flour mixed with liquid from the can of mushrooms to the pan drippings. Add green onions, parsley, and mushrooms. Cook for 5 minutes, stirring until slightly thickened. Pour over meat in a large serving bowl. Serve over steamed rice. Yields 8 servings.

Makes a heap of biscuits. Store the extras in the freezer to use as needed.

This is by far my favorite camp recipe.

75

TURTLE STEW

3 pounds turtle meat
3 tablespoons margarine
3 tablespoons all-purpose flour
3 onions, chopped
2 cloves garlic, minced
2 bell peppers, finely chopped
1 (6 oz.) can tomato paste
2 (14 1/2 oz.) cans tomatoes
Boiling water
1 rib celery, finely chopped

1 bunch green onions, chopped
Tony's Creole Seasoning
1/2 cup Sherry wine
4 bay leaves
8 whole cloves
1/2 teaspoon powdered allspice
1 tablespoon sugar
6 hard-boiled eggs
1 lemon, sliced
1/4 pound butter

In a pot, boil the turtle meat for 15 minutes. In a Dutch oven, make a brown roux of margarine and flour. Add onions, garlic, bell pepper, tomato paste, and tomatoes. Cook slowly 20 to 30 minutes. Add turtle meat, along with enough boiling water to cover meat. Bring to a boil and boil for 15 minutes. Add celery, green onions, Tony's Creole Seasoning, wine, bay leaves, cloves, allspice, and sugar. Cover and cook over medium heat for 30 minutes. Mash egg yolks; chop the whites. Add to stew. If stew gets too thick, add a little water. Simmer for 1 hour. Thirty minutes before serving, add sliced lemon and butter. Yields 6 servings.

MCJUNKIN'S TURTLE SAUCE PIQUANTE

3 pounds turtle meat

Tony's Creole Seasoning

8 tablespoons margarine

2 cups basic vegetable mixture
  (pg. 25)

1 (3 oz.) can button mushrooms

1(6 oz.) can mushroom steak sauce

1 (10 oz.) can Rotel tomatoes

1 long green hot pepper, chopped

2 cups water

½ cup chopped green onions

¼ cup chopped parsley

In a pot, boil meat for 15 minutes. Drain and season with Tony's Creole Seasoning. Melt margarine in a Dutch oven and brown meat until it starts to stick to the bottom. Add vegetable mixture and cook for 10 minutes. Add mushrooms, steak sauce, Rotel, pepper, and water. Bring to a boil; lower heat, cover and simmer for 3 to 4 hours until meat is tender. If gravy is too thin add a mixture of 1 tablespoon of flour and 1 cup of water. Cook until it thickens, then add green onions and parsley and serve over steamed rice. Yields 6 servings.

My friend, McJunkin, came to this area on a mule. He was a dyed-in-the-wool Arkansas red neck, but he sure could cook a mean turtle sauce piquante.

FROGMAN MARKS

Folks in south Louisiana love their frog legs--especially fried. In some seafood restaurants, it's one of the featured items of the Seafood Platter, an entree that's a combination of everything the house can fry.

My friend George Marks was the record breaker when it came to frogging. I sold him life insurance. He sold me used auto parts and told me of his escapades with frogs.

We nicknamed George the "Human Salamander." Equipped with two long poles, a back pack, a hardhat with a headlight, and his pistol, George would set out for his midnight hunt. He used the two long poles to balance himself atop the big lilies of the Boagni Swamp.

His record was 76 frogs in one night, all caught with his bare hands. For his efforts, ole George garnered 15 cents per frog, a handsome sum back then for his moonlight catch. The next day they all ended up as the Frog Leg Special on the menu at Soileau's Restaurant.

To this day, I can't enjoy frog legs without recounting the tale of the Human Salamander.

FRIED FROG LEGS

½ gallon water
½ cup lemon juice
1 teaspoon salt
12 frog legs

Tony's Creole Seasoning
2 eggs
1 cup bread crumbs
Oil for frying

Fill a pot with water: add lemon juice and salt. Bring to a boil. Scald frog legs about 3 minutes in the boiling water. Remove, dry with clean towel and season with Tony's Creole Seasoning. Dip in well beaten eggs, then roll in bread crumbs. Coat frog legs well and deep fry in 350°oil until golden brown. Remove from oil and drain well on absorbent paper. Yields 6 servings.

CREOLE-STYLE ALLIGATOR

4 tablespoons margarine
1½ cups chopped bell pepper
1⅓ cups chopped onions
2½ cups chopped celery
½ cup all-purpose flour
2 (28 oz.) cans tomatoes
Tony's Creole Seasoning

2 tablespoons brown sugar
3 bay leaves
8 whole cloves
⅓ teaspoon hot pepper sauce
4 pounds cubed alligator meat
1 tablespoon lemon juice
⅔ cup white wine

In a Dutch oven, melt margarine and add bell pepper, onions, and celery. Sauté for 10 minutes or until vegetables are tender. Add flour and blend thoroughly. Add tomatoes gradually, stirring constantly. Add Tony's Creole Seasoning, sugar, bay leaves, cloves, and hot pepper sauce. Bring to a boil. Add alligator meat to mixture and return to a boil. Reduce heat and simmer, uncovered, for 45 minutes, stirring occasionally. Remove from heat; discard bay leaves and cloves. Stir in lemon juice and wine. Serve over steamed rice. Yields 15 servings.

RUSSELL GREEN'S ROLLED ALLIGATOR ROAST

Russell Green of Kaplan, LA, a prominent Brahma cattle breeder and an outstanding sportsman, taught me this method. I believe that this is the finest way of all to cook alligator.

I've even cooked it in the Cajun microwave. Ah, superb!

1 alligator tail fillet
Tony's Creole Seasoning
2 onions, chopped
3 bell peppers, chopped
2 cloves garlic, minced

String
4 tablespoons margarine
6 slices bacon
1 cup white wine

Season fillet generously with Tony's Creole Seasoning. In a small bowl, make a mixture of onions, bell pepper, and garlic. Sprinkle mixture down the length of the fillet. Roll the fillet and tie with string in about 4 places to hold in place.

Melt margarine in a Dutch oven. Place roast in Dutch oven and cover with slices of bacon. Heat oven to 450° and cook roast until bacon is crisp. Pour wine over roast; reduce oven to 300°. Cover and cook about 2 hours or until tender. Yields 8 servings.

TONY'S ALLIGATOR SAUCE PIQUANTE

3 pounds alligator meat, cut up
Tony's Creole Seasoning
8 tablespoons margarine
3 cups basic vegetable mixture
   (pg. 25)
1 (8 oz.) can tomato sauce

1 (10 oz.) can Rotel tomatoes
1/2 teaspoon sugar
1/4 cup Tony's Roux and
   Gravy Mix
1 cup Burgundy wine
Water to cover meat

Season meat generously with Tony's Creole Seasoning. In a Dutch oven, fry meat in melted margarine. Add basic vegetable mixture; cook for 5 minutes or until vegetables are tender. Add tomato sauce, Rotel tomatoes, and sugar. Cook another 5 minutes, stirring constantly. In a measuring cup, dissolve Tony's Roux and Gravy Mix with wine and add to pot. Add enough water to cover meat. Bring to a boil, then simmer for 3 to 4 hours until meat is tender and gravy is at desired consistency. Adjust seasoning and serve over steamed rice. Yields 8 servings.

JIM BOWIE'S GARFISH BOULETTES

3 pounds garfish meat
2 onions, chopped
8 potatoes, peeled and boiled
1 egg
1/2 cup chopped green onions

1/2 cup chopped parsley
Tony's Creole Seasoning
2 cups all-purpose flour
Oil for frying

Clean garfish. With a fork, scrape off meat so as to separate the gristle. Grind onions and meat and place in a large bowl. In a separate bowl mash potatoes. Add mashed potatoes, egg, green onions, and parsley to the meat mixture. Blend well. Season with Tony's Creole Seasoning. Roll into 1 inch balls; dip in flour, and deep fry in 375° oil until golden brown. Yields 10 servings.

You haven't eaten gator till you've eaten it made this way. Strictly for the serious eater!

These boulettes are delicious in courtbouillon or to serve as is.

JOE'S CAMP AT THE POINT

My brother Joe married into the Beaullieu family of Lafayette, a family who had one of the very first camps on the "Cajun Riviera," also known as Cypremort Point. Located 20 miles south of New Iberia on Vermilion Bay, the peninsula is called Cypremort, meaning "dead cypress," because its cypress trees died as salt water invaded the area. Hundreds of camps now line the coast at the Point.

Joe and his wife Helen built a huge getaway on Cypremort Point back in the late 1950s. Some weekends were family weekends. Others were fishing weekends just for the menfolk. I was often invited on "men only" weekends because the fellows loved my cooking.

We usually ate a big breakfast before setting out for a day on the water. My breakfast spread usually included Heavenly Eggs, bacon or sausage, grits, hot biscuits with fig preserves, and strong Cajun coffee. After a breakfast like that, nobody was hungry until the afternoon!

Before heading out, one of us was in charge of baiting the crab traps which dangled off Joe's pier near the camp. It usually took us an hour after breakfast to get our gear together, board Joe's big salt water rig and cross the choppy waters of Vermilion Bay to Southwest Pass. That's where the bay meets the Gulf of Mexico.

If you think Louisiana summers are hot, try being out on open water in the dead of summer with the sun beating down on you and no shade for miles. Fortunately, the Gulf always provided a bounty of fish to make the parched lips and sunburns worth our while. We'd fish for hours trying to find the spot where we could hook the prettiest redfish and speckled trout, one after the other. As each shiny, squirming fighter was tossed into the live well, I imagined him filleted and stuffed, baking in seasonings and wine.

Back at the Point those afternoons, we'd rotate turns cleaning fish, showering, and napping before prepping our fresh catch for supper. A check of the crab traps usually turned up eight to ten dozen pretty blue point crabs to add to our fine meal.

Occasionally, the waters were too rough to venture out to the Gulf, so I always brought something else to cook, just in case. I remember a great squirrel dinner once and another time it was my famous Teal with Oysters. But the fresh catch, when we were able to fish, usually became an entree of Baked Red Snapper with Crab and Shrimp Stuffing. Man, that was good eating.

Even worth a sunburn.

GRILLED SNAPPER

4 tablespoons margarine
3 tablespoons chopped onion
1 tablespoon chopped bell pepper
2 tablespoons minced parsley

1 teaspoon hot pepper sauce
2 lemons, sliced
Tony's Creole Seasoning
1 (6 lb.) whole red snapper

Melt margarine in a saucepan. Add all ingredients except fish; stir well to mix. Place snapper on a sheet of heavy foil and pour sauce over fish. Seal foil, making sure there is no leakage. Place on a grill with a hood, if possible. Turn every 10 minutes, being careful not to tear the foil. Cook for 30 minutes. Open foil, drain and reserve liquid. Cook another 10 minutes, basting with the liquid. Yields 6 servings.

TONY'S
FISH COURTBOUILLON

1 cup all-purpose flour
1 cup margarine
3 cups basic vegetable mixture
 (pg. 25)
1 (6 oz.) can tomato paste
1 (8 oz.) can tomato sauce

8 cups water
½ lemon, sliced
1 (8 lb.) fish, cut in pieces
Tony's Creole Seasoning
½ cup chopped green onions

In a Dutch oven, make a dark roux with flour and margarine. Remove from heat and add basic vegetable mixture, stirring mixture until it stops sizzling. Add tomato paste and tomato sauce. Stir over low heat for 5 minutes. Add water; stir well and bring to a boil. Add lemon slices. Lower heat; cover and simmer for 2 hours, stirring occasionally to prevent sticking on bottom.

Season fish with Tony's Creole Seasoning; add to mixture. Bring to a boil; lower heat, cover and simmer for 30 minutes. Add more water if the sauce is too thick. Add green onions. Serve over steamed rice. Yields 10 servings.

Serve this snapper with grilled Parmesan corn and salad greens.

I recommend using any large fresh water fish for this fine Creole dish.

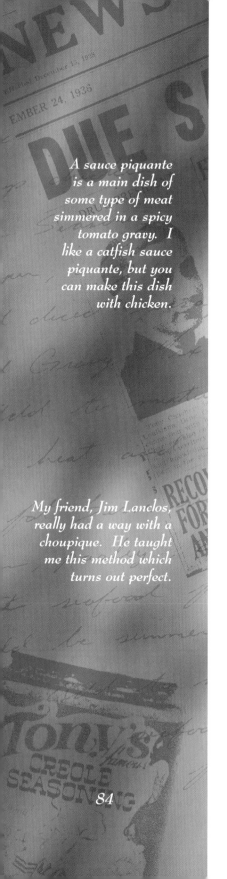

A sauce piquante is a main dish of some type of meat simmered in a spicy tomato gravy. I like a catfish sauce piquante, but you can make this dish with chicken.

My friend, Jim Lanclos, really had a way with a choupique. He taught me this method which turns out perfect.

CATFISH SAUCE PIQUANTE

6 tablespoons margarine
1 cup chopped onion
1 cup chopped bell pepper
¼ cup chopped green onions
1 (8 oz.) can tomato sauce

1 (10 oz.) can diced tomatoes
   with green chilies
6 pounds catfish fillets, cut up
Tony's Creole Seasoning

Melt margarine in a 2 quart pot over medium heat. Sauté onion and bell pepper in margarine. Add green onions. When vegetables are tender, add tomato sauce and diced tomatoes with green chilies. Simmer for 1 hour. Season fish with Tony's Creole Seasoning and add to the sauce; simmer for 20 minutes. Serve over steamed rice. Yields 6 servings.

JIM'S CHOUPIQUE
Bayou Courtableau Style

1 (8 lb.) choupique, filleted
Tony's Creole Seasoning
½ cup oil
2 onions, chopped
1 bell pepper, chopped
8 garlic cloves, chopped
1 (8 oz.) can tomato sauce

1 (10 oz.) can Rotel tomatoes
2 cups water
½ lemon, sliced
1 (4 oz.) can mushrooms
½ cup chopped green onions
¼ cup chopped parsley

Cut fillets into small pieces. Season with Tony's Creole Seasoning and fry in oil in Dutch oven until firm. Remove fillets from the oil. Add onions, bell pepper, and garlic to the oil; sauté until tender. Add tomato sauce, Rotel tomatoes, and water. Add fillets and bring to a boil. Reduce heat and simmer for 45 minutes. Do not stir; instead, gently lift the pot off the burner with both hands and tilt it from side to side. Do this once or twice during cooking to prevent fillets from breaking apart. Add lemon slices, mushrooms, green onions, and parsley; cook over low heat for another 15 minutes. Serve over steamed rice. Yields 6 servings.

DRIED SHRIMP

1 cup salt
5 bay leaves
5 cloves garlic
1 bottle beer

8 cups water
5 pounds small shrimp
2 foot strip cheese cloth

Place first 5 ingredients in a large pot. Bring to a rolling boil; add the shrimp. Lower heat and boil for 3 to 4 minutes; remove from heat and let stand for 2 minutes. Drain and peel shrimp. Place cheese cloth on cookie sheet and spread shrimp in a single layer. Cover with cheese cloth; place in sun for 2 to 3 days, away from the ground. You may also place the shrimp in a 200° oven for 6 to 8 hours. Yields about 2 quarts.

CRAB STEW

12 medium crabs, cleaned
4 tablespoons all-purpose flour
4 tablespoons margarine
1 onion, minced
1/2 bell pepper, chopped

1(14 1/2 oz.) can stewed tomatoes
2 cloves garlic, minced
2 sprigs parsley, chopped
2 green onions, chopped
Tony's Creole Seasoning

In a Dutch oven, melt margarine and stir in flour to make a brown roux. Add onions and bell pepper. When onions have become transparent, add other ingredients. Season with Tony's Creole Seasoning. Cook about 30 minutes on low heat. Add crabs. Cook in gravy for 30 minutes. If gravy becomes too thick, add water to desired consistency. Serve over steamed rice. Yields 4 servings.

Good for adding to a gumbo or soup and will keep in a jar stored in a dry, cool place for months.

Potato salad would be great with this stew.

85

THE CAMP ON
THE BIG ALABAMA

Back in early 1932, I made my first fishing trip down the Big Alabama, a small bayou below Krotz Springs. The area was teeming with wildlife back then. My catch that trip included bass, white perch, bream, gaspergou, blue crabs, and plenty crawfish. After that trip, four friends and I pledged to build ourselves a camp out there.

We built our camp eight miles by boat down the bayou from the Krotz Springs landing. Getting there sometimes proved to be quite an adventure in itself. Often the bayou filled up with water lilies, making it virtually impassable. Water in the bayou was so low at times that we got hopelessly stuck in mud. Once we'd finally arrive, we were sure glad to see our weekend home away from home.

The camp was quite a haven for the 1930s. It had a cistern for collecting drinking and cooking water. Our bathing water we drew from the bayou. Butane provided power for our lights. A brick hearth encased our fire for cooking.

I remember putting many a soup to cooking in that fireplace on chilly mornings before setting out to fish. Squirrel stew, fish courtbouillon, wild ducks, soft-shell turtles, and tasty swamp rabbits were among my favorites cooked at the camp. We only cooked what we killed out in the marsh or caught in the bayou.

A flood in the mid 1930s filled the camp with three feet of sand. At that point, I became sole proprietor of the camp, the only one of the five of us who returned to get things going again after the flood. My family and I continued to enjoy our camp on the Big Alabama until the mid 1980s.

Probably my all-time favorite memories over the 50 years on the Big Alabama are of rainy nights spent roasting pecans and brewing hot buttered rum in that cozy hearth. A big rocking chair, the warm drink, the aroma of the roasting nuts, raindrops falling on the roof...nothing could be better.

BIG ALABAMA BAYOU ROASTED PECANS AND HOT BUTTERED RUM

Roasted Pecans

Melt enough butter in a frying pan to coat. Add pecans, sprinkled with a little salt, and fry until slightly brown. Delicious with hot, buttered rum...while sitting in a rocking chair...in front of a roaring fire...raindrops falling on the roof....

Hot Buttered Rum

1 pat butter

1 jigger rum

1 teaspoon sugar

1 teaspoon lemon juice

Dash cinnamon

1 cup boiling water

Place butter in a mug. Add rum, sugar, and lemon juice. Add water and sprinkle with cinnamon. Yields 1 serving.

TONY'S VENISON CHOPS

4 large shoulder venison chops

Tony's Creole Seasoning

2 tablespoons oil

1 cup honey

1 cup dry white wine

1 clove garlic, minced

$\frac{1}{2}$ teaspoon ginger

Season chops with Tony's Creole Seasoning and brown slowly, in a Dutch oven, on both sides in oil. In a bowl, combine remaining ingredients, mixing thoroughly. Pour over chops. Simmer for 45 minutes or until tender. Serve chops and sauce over steamed rice. Yields 4 servings.

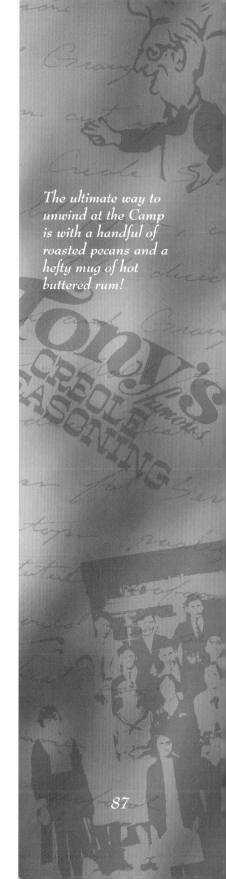

The ultimate way to unwind at the Camp is with a handful of roasted pecans and a hefty mug of hot buttered rum!

VENISON STEW

3 pounds venison, cubed
Tony's Creole Seasoning
3 tablespoons oil
4 tablespoons all-purpose flour
1 bell pepper, chopped
3 ribs celery, chopped

2 onions, chopped
6 green onions, chopped
½ pound carrots, chopped
¼ teaspoon thyme
1 bay leaf, crushed

In a heavy pot, season venison with Tony's Creole Seasoning and sauté in oil until brown. Remove meat and stir flour into hot oil, making a roux. Stir until roux is dark brown. Lower heat and add bell pepper, celery, onions, and green onions to roux and sauté for 3 minutes. Add water slowly to make a gravy, stirring constantly. Return meat and remaining ingredients to gravy. Mix thoroughly. Cover and simmer for 3 hours or until tender. Serve over steamed rice. Yields 8 servings.

Talk about good on a cold winter night!

TONY'S CAS-CA-RA

3 pounds navy beans
4 tablespoons margarine
3 cups basic vegetable mixture (pg. 25)

1 pounds boiled ham, diced
Tony's Creole Seasoning

In a Dutch oven, boil beans in salted water until tender and strain through a colander. In the same pot, melt margarine; add vegetable mixture. Sauté for 10 minutes. Add ham; sauté for 10 minutes. Add beans and enough water to make a thick sauce. Season with Tony's Creole Seasoning. Simmer for 1 hour. Add more water if needed. Serve in soup bowls with corn bread. Yields 12 servings.

TONY'S
HE-MAN CHILI

1 pound hot sausage (Louisiana or Italian)
1 pound lean ground beef
1 onion, chopped
1 bell pepper, chopped
2 cloves garlic, minced
1 Louisiana hot green pepper, or Jalapeño, diced
1 cup Burgundy wine
1 teaspoon dry mustard
1 teaspoon celery seeds
2 tablespoons chili powder
3 cups chopped Roma tomatoes
Tony's Creole Seasoning
1 (15 ½ oz.) can pinto beans
2 (15 ½ oz.) cans kidney beans

Slice sausage into 1 inch pieces and fry in a Dutch oven until brown. Remove and set aside. Pour off excess fat and fry ground beef. Drain and set aside with the sausage. Pour excess fat from pot. Cook onions, bell pepper, garlic, and hot pepper over low heat until tender. Stir in wine, mustard, celery seeds, and chili powder. Simmer for 10 minutes. In a bowl, mash tomatoes; pour into pot. Add meats. Bring to a boil. Reduce heat; season with Tony's Creole Seasoning. Simmer for 30 minutes, stirring occasionally. Add beans and their liquid; return to a boil. Reduce heat and simmer for 1 hour, stirring occasionally. Yields 12 servings.

RICE STEAMER
BEEF AND CABBAGE

1 pound ground meat
1 pound smoked sausage, sliced
1 medium head cabbage, chopped
1 onion, chopped
1 bell pepper, chopped
1 (10 oz.) can Rotel tomatoes
½ cup rice
½ cup water
Tony's Creole Seasoning
Cooking spray

Mix all ingredients in a rice steamer coated with cooking spray. Cook and allow to continue steaming 20 minutes after the "cook" button goes off. Yields 8 portions.

This one'll put hair on your chest!

Here in south Louisiana, every home has a rice steamer. I dare say every camp and motor home's got one too! This is an easy meal, no matter where you cook it.

89

"A group of us got together...to officially incorporate and finance the first Yambilee celebration in 1946."

FESTIVE COOKING

LET'S HAVE A YAMBILEE

I've compiled quite a collection of yam recipes over the years because of my connection to our local yam festival, the Yambilee.

The festival started on the suggestion of J. W. "Bill" Low, a fellow who transferred to Opelousas from east Texas. Back in his hometown, there was an annual festival called Jubilee. During that era, many south Louisiana communities were developing annual events to promote their community's most vital resource. Yams were big business in our Creole town, so it was only natural that we chose to honor yam farming as our No. 1 industry.

A group of us got together with Bill Low to officially incorporate and finance the first Yambilee celebration in 1946. In only a few years, the event grew from a one-day cooking and eating contest to a three-day weekend of floats and parades, a street fair, a fais-do-do, and a Miss Yambilee. There was even a group of lady singers called the Yamettes.

I've been awfully proud of the great cooks of our community who've been creating some really tasty dishes with yams, but it's the kids' creations that I enjoy most. I'm invited every year to judge the yam cooking contests. When I can make it, I choose the kids' division.

I've chosen a few of my favorite recipes from among the Yambilee winners over the years to include in this book. But if you can make the trip, our Yambilee's still held the last weekend of every October.

FESTIVE COOKING
Contents

BLOODY MARY

1 ounce vodka
4 ounce tomato juice
Dash of Worcestershire sauce
Dash of hot pepper sauce

Dash of celery salt
Dash of lemon juice
Tony's Creole Seasoning

Combine all ingredients and shake in cocktail shaker. Rim glass with Tony's Creole Seasoning; fill glass with ice and pour mixture into glass. Garnish with celery, pickled okra, or pickled string bean. Yields 1 serving.

BULL SHOT

2 parts vodka
2 parts beef broth
Dash lemon juice

Dash Worcestershire sauce
Pinch of Tony's Creole Seasoning
Dash hot pepper sauce

Stir ingredients with a spoon and pour into glass filled with ice cubes. Yields 1 serving.

MIMOSA

Orange juice, chilled until slushy   Champagne, blush

Pour equal parts of champagne and orange juice into a champagne flute. Garnish with an orange slice or mint leaf. Serve immediately.

In many restaurants, I've seen bartenders use my seasoning to make Bloody Marys. Guess the word got around.

What a great drink for a champagne brunch! I recommend Mimosa with my French Omelet.

95

MINT JULEP

4 sprigs fresh mint	Cracked ice
1 teaspoon powdered sugar	3 jiggers bourbon

Mash mint leaves and sugar in bottom of an "old–fashion" glass. Fill with cracked ice. Pour in bourbon. Stir until glass frosts. Garnish with a sprig of mint. Yields 1 serving.

POUSSE CAFÉ

1. Grenadine
2. Maraschino
3. Green Creme de Menthe
4. Creme de Violette
5. Chartreuse
6. Brandy

In the order listed above, pour an equal amount of each liqueur into a slender glass, forming a stack of layers. Yields 1 serving.

SAZERAC COCKTAIL

3 dashes anisette	1 cube sugar
1 jigger bourbon	1 dash orange bitters
Twist of lemon	1 dash Angostura bitters

Place ingredients in cocktail shaker. Shake well and pour into "old–fashion" glass with plenty of cracked ice. Add a twist of lemon and serve. Yields 1 serving.

RED ROOSTER

1 pint vodka

1 (6 oz.) can frozen orange juice

1 quart cranberry juice

Juice of 1 lemon

In a bowl, mix all ingredients and freeze. Before serving, whirl in blender. Pour into chilled "old–fashion" glass. Garnish with lemon slice. Yields 8 one–cup servings.

HURRICANE

1 pint dark rum

½ cup lemon juice

1 cup Hawaiian Punch® concentrate

Crushed ice

Fresh fruit

In a cocktail shaker, blend together rum, lemon juice, and punch base. Pour equal portions into tall glasses filled with crushed ice. Garnish with orange or lemon slice and stemmed cherry. Yields 4 cocktails.

BLACKBERRY WINE

4 quarts blackberries

Boiling water to cover

3½ pounds brown sugar

In a large pot, cover blackberries with boiling water and let stand for 2 hours. Strain berry juice through a cheesecloth, then add sugar to the liquid. Pour liquid in an open jar; cover with cheese cloth and let stand until fermenting ceases. Then bottle. Simple! Yields 2 quarts.

This blackberry wine takes about 2 months to ferment, but the result is worth the wait!

TEA PUNCH

1 pint tea	1 pint pineapple juice
4 cups sugar	1 (20 oz.) can fruit cocktail
1 pint water	2 quarts ginger ale, chilled
1 pint lemonade	3 gallons cold water
1 pint orange juice	Small jar cherries

In a pot, brew a pint of strong tea. In a saucepan, make a syrup by bringing sugar and water to a boil. Pour the syrup into a gallon container. Add the tea, lemonade, and juices. Stir to blend. Chill until ready to serve. Pour fruit cocktail into a tube or Bundt pan. Fill pan with some of the punch mixture and freeze for ice ring. At party time, set frozen punch ring in punch bowl. In 5 gallon container, mix gallon of punch with ginger ale, water, and cherries with juice. Pour to fill bowl. Replenish as needed. Yields 6 dozen one cup servings.

WILD CHERRY BOUNCE

1 quart wild cherries	1 fifth bourbon
1 pound sugar	

Wash and pick over cherries, removing stems. Drain. Place moist cherries in a half–gallon jug. Pour ½ cup sugar over moist cherries, then shake until cherries are coated. Pour remaining sugar on top of cherries. Do not mix. Place cap on jug loosely to prevent pressure buildup. Let stand until sugar melts on top of cherries, then stir by revolving the jug. Repeat until sugar is dissolved.

Let stand for 2 months. Pour bourbon over cherries and close jug tightly. Let stand 3 or 4 months. During this time, revolve jug occasionally. Strain through cheese cloth and pour into bottles. Yields ½ gallon.

DROP IN AT HOOK INN

Many festive times were enjoyed by friends I hosted at Hook Inn.

Old Hook Inn was a camp behind my house back in the 1950s and 1960s. It was part of the old Cedar Lane Club that I bought and hauled onto my property. It was a two-story structure which I positioned to overlook a coulee. It had one big room on the bottom with a stove and sink and a big counter. Upstairs was one large room with big windows on all four sides. It was typical of many camps like folks have out at Holly Beach.

We used to have lots of parties there. I entertained many insurance customers during that time and had a meal up there about every other week. Sometimes I hosted my Cooks Unlimited group up there.

My friend, Vincent Moseley, called it "Goat Castle," probably because when we gathered together for an all-male evening, we had a tendency to be pretty rowdy.

We had one friend, Pap, whose wife didn't approve of our loud evenings of bourré, cigars, and beer. One particular stormy night, we invited Pap to join us for a sauce piquant. Despite protests from the Mrs., Pap insisted that he take his pirogue down to Hook Inn so that he could "rescue" us from the rising water.

We periodically had Ladies' Night at Hook Inn, a night where our wives had the night off from the kitchen while us fellows treated them to our culinary talents. We really pulled out all the stops on Ladies' Night as we were eager to show the gals how handy we could be with a cleaver and a hen.

When I needed a place to get away, Hook Inn was the spot. No telephone, no radio, no frills. I could cook back there in peace.

One night in the late 1960s, Hook Inn burned to the ground. I never built another one. I'm always surprised by the people that remember it, though. So often, a friend will say, "Remember that time at Hook Inn....", and I nod and recall the same event.

Ah, sweet memories.

These treats will keep
for 2 to 3 weeks.

WHISKEY BALLS

2 cups crushed vanilla wafers
1 cup confectioners sugar
2 jiggers whiskey

2 cups ground pecans
3 tablespoons white corn syrup

In a small bowl, mix all ingredients together and shape into 1 inch
balls. If mixture is too dry add a little more syrup. Roll in extra
confectioners sugar. Store in container with tight–fitting lid until
ready to serve. Yields 30 balls.

DATE BALLS

8 tablespoons margarine
1 pound chopped dates
1 cup shredded coconut
1 cup dark brown sugar

1 cup light brown sugar
4 cups Rice Krispies®
2 cups chopped pecans
1 cup confectioners sugar

Cook margarine, dates, coconut, and sugars in a saucepan over low
heat. Let come to a bubble, then cook for 6 minutes. Add cereal
and pecans. Make small balls and roll in confectioners sugar.
Yields 3 dozen balls.

CHEESE BISCUITS

Recipe may be doubled
or tripled as needed.

4 tablespoons margarine
1 cup shredded sharp
  Cheddar cheese
1 cup shredded mild
  Cheddar cheese

1 cup all-purpose flour
Tony's Creole Seasoning
1 clove garlic, minced

In a large bowl, cream margarine and cheeses. Add flour, Tony's
Creole Seasoning, and garlic. Roll into tiny balls, the size of
marbles. Bake at 400° for 15 minutes. Biscuits may be frozen
and baked while still frozen. Yields 30 to 36 biscuits.

PRALINES AU BÉNÉ

2 cups sesame seeds
1/2 cup milk
4 tablespoons margarine

2 cups sugar
Pinch of salt
2 teaspoons corn syrup

Stir sesame seeds in a Dutch oven or skillet over medium heat until parched light brown. In a saucepan, heat milk, margarine, sugar, salt, and syrup. Cook to soft–ball stage. Remove from heat and stir until thick. Add parched seeds and stir until well mixed. Pour mixture into pancake–size portions on well–greased cookie sheet or waxed paper and cool. Yields 10 servings.

OPELOUSAS PRALINES

2 cups sugar
Pinch of salt
1 (5 oz.) can evaporated milk

2 tablespoons sugar
2 teaspoons vanilla extract
3 cups pecan halves

In one pot, mix sugar, salt, and milk. Cook to soft–ball stage (test by dropping a little in water). Remove from heat.

While the above is cooking, caramelize 2 heaping tablespoons sugar in a small, thick skillet until brown. Pour sugar into liquid mixture after it reaches test stage. Stir, then remove from heat. Add vanilla and pecans; beat. Before candy crystallizes, dip out by spoonfuls and place on waxed paper to cool. If mixture should crystallize too soon (before removing from pot), add a tablespoon of boiling water and beat again. Yields 3 dozen pralines.

One hundred years ago, this was a big treat for the children, especially during lean times. They're still a family favorite.

My buddy, Hugh, got this recipe from his teacher, Mrs. Alice Dietlein Moore, back when he was a student in her class. Pralines were the ultimate treat when we were children. When I pick a bucketful of pecans from the huge trees in my yard each fall, pralines are still the first thing I look forward to making with them.

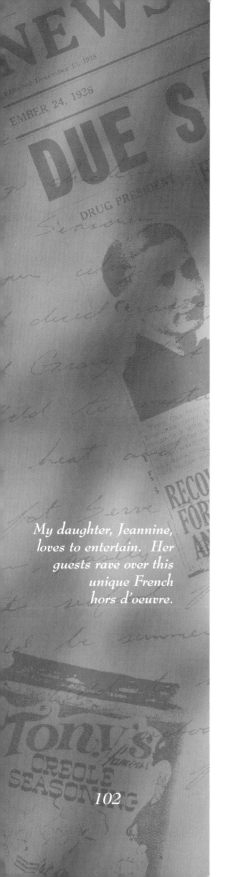

YAM COOKIES

1 cup sugar
1 cup margarine
1/2 cup mashed yams
1 egg

2 1/2 cups all-purpose flour
1/4 teaspoon salt
1 teaspoon vanilla extract
Apricot jam

In a large bowl, cream sugar and margarine together. Add yams. Mix thoroughly. Add egg and beat with mixer for 2 minutes at medium speed. Add flour sifted with salt. Add vanilla. Mix thoroughly. Drop by teaspoonful onto greased baking sheet 2 inches apart. Press flat with fork and make depression in middle with finger. Put a dab of apricot jam in depression. Bake at 375° for 10 minutes. Yields 5 to 6 dozen cookies.

HOME-STYLE BOURSIN

2 (8 oz.) packages cream cheese, softened
1/4 cup mayonnaise
2 teaspoons Dijon mustard

2 tablespoons chopped chives
2 tablespoons dill weed
1 clove garlic, minced

In a bowl, mix all ingredients together. For party spread, simply spread on favorite little party breads. For party ball, shape into a ball and roll in 1/2 cup crushed pecans. Wrap in clear wrap and refrigerate for 3 days. Serve on cheese board with favorite breads or crackers.

My daughter, Jeannine, loves to entertain. Her guests rave over this unique French hors d'oeuvre.

PICKLED
SNAP BEANS

1 pound (6 inches) snap beans
1 cup chopped onions
2 cups sugar

3 cups water
1 cup vinegar

In a pan, boil snap beans in salted water for 10 minutes. Drain and place in pint jars (about 4). Distribute chopped onions to each jar. Combine sugar, water, and vinegar in a saucepan. Boil for 5 minutes, then pour over snap beans and onions in each jar. Seal jars. Yields 4 pints.

PICKLED OKRA

4 pounds small tender okra
10 pods red or green peppers
  (Louisiana Red Hots)
10 cloves garlic
8 cups vinegar

1 cup water
3/4 cup salt
Celery salt or mustard seed,
  optional

Wash okra; leave stems on. Pack in pint jars (about 10), stems up. Place 1 pepper pod and 1 garlic clove in each jar. In a pot, bring vinegar, water, and salt to a boil; remove from heat immediately. Add 1 teaspoon celery salt or mustard seed, if desired. Pour hot mixture over okra and seal jars. Let stand 2 months before using. Yields 10 pints.

Pickled snap beans make a perfect swizzle stick for a Cajun Bloody Mary. Down here, we call them "les haricots," (pronounced lay-zah-dee-koh).

Pickled okra are as welcome on the party relish tray as they are everyday on the kitchen table.

CREOLE SEAFOOD SAUCE

Makes an excellent condiment for shrimp cocktail and oysters on the half shell.

1 cup catsup
1 tablespoon horseradish
1 teaspoon Worcestershire sauce

1 tablespoon hot pepper sauce
1/2 cup celery, finely chopped
Tony's Creole Seasoning

In a small bowl, mix all ingredients. Bottle and chill. Serve as a condiment with your favorite boiled shellfish. Yields about 1½ cups.

CRAB MEAT DIP

3 tablespoons butter
1/2 cup all-purpose flour
1/8 teaspoon prepared mustard
Tony's Creole Seasoning

3 cups milk
1/2 pound shredded sharp
  Cheddar cheese
1 pound lump crab meat

Melt butter in a double boiler. Stir in flour, mustard, and Tony's Creole Seasoning. Blend well. Add milk to mixture gradually. Stir constantly until thickened. Add cheese, stirring until melted. Fold in crab meat and heat about 5 minutes, stirring occasionally. Pour into chafing dish. Yields 4 dozen small canape shells.

MUSHROOMS STUFFED
WITH CRAB MEAT

8 large mushrooms
1 cup lump crab meat
1 tablespoon bread crumbs
1 tablespoon chopped onions
Tony's Creole Seasoning

2 tablespoons chopped parsley
1 egg, slightly beaten
Bread crumbs
Parmesan cheese

Rinse mushrooms and remove stems. In a bowl, mix crab meat with
bread crumbs, onion, Tony's Creole Seasoning, and parsley. Add egg
and mix well. Fill mushroom caps with mixture and sprinkle with
bread crumbs and cheese. Place in 350° oven until light brown.
Yields 8 mushrooms.

BROILED SHRIMP
A LA TONY

12 large shrimp, peeled
1 clove garlic, minced
2 tablespoons lemon juice

Tony's Creole Seasoning
½ cup olive oil

Slit shrimp down back, cutting ¾ way through to remove sand veins,
leaving tail on. In a bowl, marinate shrimp for 2 hours in mixture
of remaining ingredients. Place shrimp in a broiling pan and pour
marinade over shrimp. Broil 5 minutes, turning once. Serve as an
appetizer. Yields 4 servings.

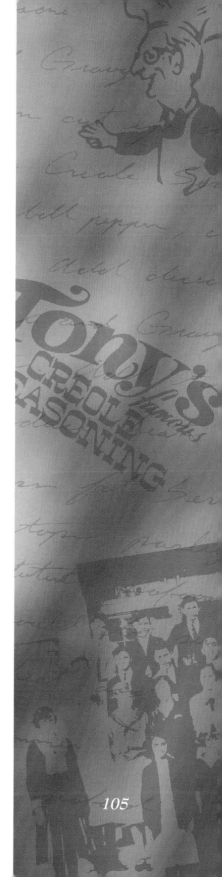

HUITRES AU DIABLE
Deviled Oysters

3 dozen oysters
1 tablespoon margarine
2 tablespoons all-purpose flour
1 cup cream
2 egg yolks, well beaten
1 tablespoon minced parsley
1 bay leaf, crushed

1/4 teaspoon thyme
Tony's Creole Seasoning
Bread crumbs
Sprigs of parsley
Olives
Lemons

Drain and chop oysters into fine pieces. In a small bowl, mix together margarine and flour until smooth. Place cream in a saucepan and when it starts to boil, stir in margarine and flour mixture. Stirring constantly, return to a boil and allow to boil for 3 minutes. Remove from heat. Let cool; add yolks, parsley, bay leaf, thyme, oysters, and Tony's Creole Seasoning. Fill 6 ramekins with the mixture. Sprinkle lightly with bread crumbs and top with a pinch of margarine. Place in a baking pan and brown for 5 minutes in a 500° oven. Garnish with sprigs of parsley, olives, and sliced lemon. Yields 6 servings.

CHICKEN SALAD

1 hen
Tony's Creole Seasoning
Garlic cloves, optional
1 cup chicken broth
1 rib celery, finely chopped

1 hard-boiled egg, chopped
4 hard-boiled egg whites, chopped
3 medium sour pickles, diced
4 to 6 capers, mashed
Mayonnaise

Season hen with Tony's Creole Seasoning. Place in stock pot with enough water to cover and a few cloves of garlic. Boil until the hen is tender. Remove hen and debone. Cut breast into large pieces. Dice remaining parts of the hen. Place chicken pieces in a large bowl. Add 1 cup chicken broth, celery, egg, egg whites, pickles, and capers. Refrigerate 1 hour. Add mayonnaise to desired consistency. Serve on lettuce leaves. Yields 8 servings.

CREOLE STUFFED TONGUE

1 beef tongue, cleaned
Tony's Creole Seasoning
1 bell pepper, chopped
6 cloves garlic, minced

1 onion, chopped
1 carrot, length of tongue
Needle and thread
1 tablespoon oil

Cut a slit the length of the tongue. Season with Tony's Creole Seasoning and stuff with vegetables. Place carrot lengthwise in opening and sew up.

In Dutch oven, fry tongue in a little oil until brown, adding ice water as needed to keep from burning. Continue cooking for 2 hours, adding cold water as needed, and turning. When tender, slice crosswise. Yields 12 appetizer servings.

CRAWFISH AND BROCCOLI CASSEROLE

1 bunch green onions, chopped
1 bell pepper, chopped
2 tablespoons margarine
1 (6 oz.) jar cheese spread
1 (6 oz.) jar Jalapeño cheese
  spread
2 cups steamed rice

1 (10 oz.) bag chopped broccoli
1 (12 oz.) can evaporated milk
1 (10 ¾ oz.) can cream of
  mushroom soup
1 (10 ¾ oz.) can cream of
  chicken soup
1 pound crawfish tails

Sauté green onions and bell pepper in skillet using margarine. Combine all ingredients in an oblong baking dish. Bake at 350° for 45 minutes. Yields 8 servings.

This delicacy is often found at weddings and receptions here in Cajun Country. Slice thin for more servings.

"One of the little ones ran over to me
with his stocking brimming over with goodies, squealing,
'Look Paw Caw, look what Santa Claus left me!'"

HOLIDAY COOKING

CHRISTMAS MEMORIES

A few years ago, I celebrated Christmas at the home of one of my grandchildren. One of the little ones ran over to me with his stocking brimming over with goodies, squealing, "Look Paw Caw, look what Santa Claus left me!"

Pulling him up on my knee, I recalled my own Christmas stocking as a boy. "When I was little, I got an apple and an orange in my stocking, and a little 25-cent wind-up toy."

"Was that during the Depression?" one of the older kids asked.

I had to chuckle. "Every year was a Depression back then," I told him, and then I recalled for them those early days when even kids had jobs to try to make ends meet.

I especially recall the years that my brother and I worked delivering newspapers, the New Orleans Daily States early in the morning and the Times Picayune in the afternoon.

At Christmas, paper boys had a special little card to deliver with each paper that asked the customer to tip us a dime. At the end of the day, I had about six or seven dollars. I remember using my money down at the local hardware store that year to buy my first shotgun!

It's funny how no matter how poor we were, I can never remember going hungry. My Mama always knew how to stretch a soup bone! It's no wonder that my favorite part of the holidays was always the big Christmas dinner.

Our house overflowed with family. Mama's Christmas Day spread usually included a baked ham, a baked turkey, corn bread dressing, petit pois, and glazed yams. Sometimes there was even a Stuffed Snapper with Oyster Dressing.

Come to think of it, that's the same dinner my wife and I always prepared for our own family. Her special addition to the traditional meal was her Ambrosia Dessert Salad, which the grandkids always loved.

The last time my turn came to host the holiday meal at my house was Christmas 1990. I served my 67 children, grandchildren, and great grandchildren and cooked every bit of it myself. The highlight of the day was a wonderful family portrait. Every time I look at it, it reminds me of many, many wonderful meals together and I feel anticipation for Christmases yet to come.

HOLIDAY COOKING
Contents

TONY'S
ROASTED TURKEY

1 (12 to 14 lb.) turkey
Tony's Creole Seasoning
1 cup basic vegetable mixture
  (pg. 25)
8 tablespoons margarine
2 strips bacon
1 cup chicken broth

½ cup chopped green onions
½ cup chopped parsley
2 (4 oz.) cans mushroom
  stems and pieces, retain juice
1 tablespoon all-purpose flour
1 (5 oz.) jar currant jelly

Season turkey generously inside and out with Tony's Creole Seasoning. Place vegetable mixture and margarine inside turkey. Place turkey in roasting pan; place bacon strips over breast. Pour the chicken broth, half inside turkey and the other half in the bottom of the roasting pan. Cover. Place in 300° oven and bake 3 to 4 hours, steaming until tender.

Remove cover and pour off pan juices into a small saucepan. Set oven to 500° and brown turkey. Watch closely; it takes only 10 minutes. To the pan juices, add green onions, parsley, and mushrooms. In a measuring cup, add mushroom juice to flour. Mix and add to pan juices. Cook for 5 minutes until juice thickens into a beautiful brown gravy. Add currant jelly if you like your gravy a little sweet. Yields 10 servings.

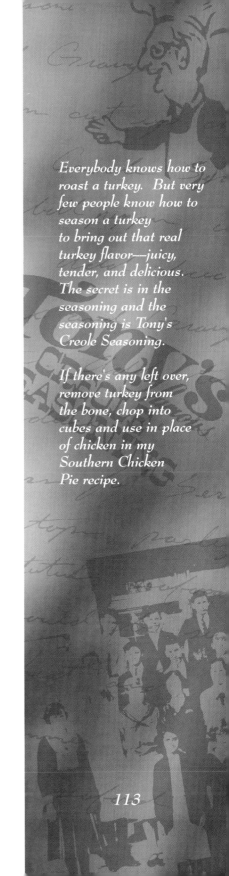

Everybody knows how to roast a turkey. But very few people know how to season a turkey to bring out that real turkey flavor—juicy, tender, and delicious. The secret is in the seasoning and the seasoning is Tony's Creole Seasoning.

If there's any left over, remove turkey from the bone, chop into cubes and use in place of chicken in my Southern Chicken Pie recipe.

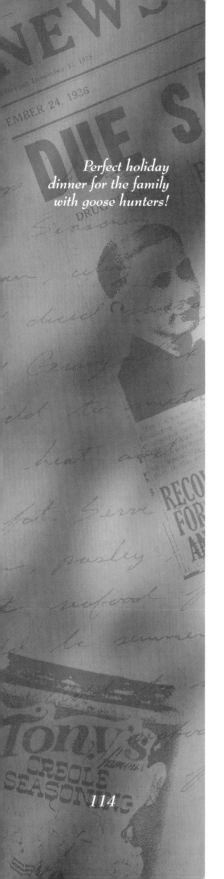

WILD GOOSE WITH GIBLET STUFFING

1 (6 to 8 lb) goose, dressed	*Tony's Creole Seasoning*
Lemon wedges	

Rub inside of goose cavity with lemon and Tony's Creole Seasoning; set aside.

Stuffing

Goose giblets	*1 onion, chopped*
2 cups water	*⅓ cup minced parsley*
10 cups crumbled corn bread	*1 to 2 tablespoons sage*
2 large Granny Smith® apples,	*Tony's Creole Seasoning*
chopped	*Margarine*

In a saucepan, cook giblets in water until tender, about 20 to 30 minutes. Remove giblets and reserve liquid. Chop giblets and place in a large bowl with the corn bread, apples, onion, parsley, sage, and Tony's Creole Seasoning. Add enough of the reserved cooking liquid to make a moist stuffing; toss gently. Stuff the body and neck cavity; close opening with skewers or needle and thread. Place goose, breast side up, on a rack in a shallow roasting pan. Spread softened margarine over the goose. Bake, uncovered, at 325° for 20 minutes per pound or until thoroughly cooked and tender. Yields 8 servings.

TONY'S BAKED PICNIC HAM

1 (8 lb.) picnic ham, deboned	1 tablespoon yellow mustard
1 tablespoon whole cloves	1/2 pound brown sugar
1 (8 oz.) can crushed pineapple	1 small jar red cherries

Have butcher debone ham and tie. Boil ham in water to cover for 1 hour. Remove skin and slice. Score with diamond–shape cuts. Stud with whole cloves. Place ham in open pan and bake in a 350° oven for 1 hour.

In a saucepan, make a glaze with a mixture of pineapple juice, mustard, and brown sugar. Cook slowly until thick.

After cooking ham, spoon glaze over ham evenly, then cover with crushed pineapple and decorate with cherries. Cook for an additional 30 minutes. Slice and serve. Yields 15 servings.

RAISIN SAUCE

2 cups water	1/4 teaspoon allspice
1 cup raisins	1/4 teaspoon cloves
1/3 cup brown sugar	1 tablespoon vinegar
1/2 teaspoon cinnamon	1/3 cup chopped pecans
2 teaspoons corn starch	1/4 teaspoon dry mustard

In a saucepan, boil water; add raisins and boil for 5 minutes. Add all other ingredients and simmer until thickened. Ladle into gravy boat or pour over baked ham. Yields 8 servings.

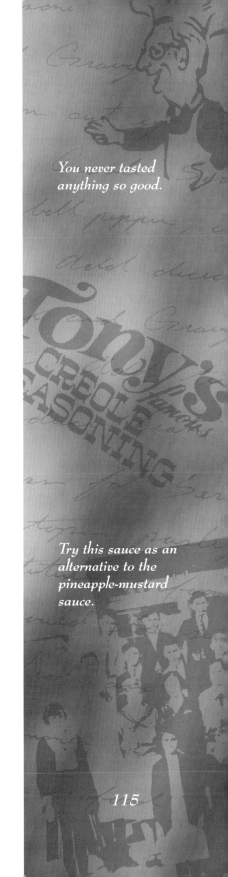

You never tasted anything so good.

Try this sauce as an alternative to the pineapple-mustard sauce.

GLAZED DUCK

1 (6 lb.) duck	1½ tablespoons vinegar
Tony's Creole Seasoning	1 cup chicken broth
¼ cup margarine	3 oranges
1 cup dry Vermouth	1 lemon
2 tablespoons sugar	2 teaspoons corn starch

Season duck with Tony's Creole Seasoning. In a Dutch oven, brown in melted margarine. Roast at 400° for 20 minutes; reduce heat to 350° and continue roasting for 1 hour. Baste frequently with Vermouth. Melt sugar in a small saucepan; add vinegar, and caramelize. Place Dutch oven on stove top. Remove duck from pot and set aside; drain fat; add chicken broth to the pan drippings. Add the juice of the oranges, a little orange zest, and the juice of a lemon. Blend in corn starch and the caramelized sugar. Cook for 10 minutes. Return duck to pot and spoon sauce over duck slowly. Heat a little longer while continuing to baste with sauce until duck is glazed. Transfer duck to serving platter and garnish with orange slices and curly parsley. Yields 4 servings.

CORN BREAD DRESSING
Tony's Special

1 pound ground chicken gizzards	2 cloves garlic, minced
½ pound lean ground pork	2 (10 ½ oz.) cans chicken broth
½ pound lean ground beef	Tony's Creole Seasoning
8 tablespoons margarine	4 cups crumbled corn bread
4 onions, chopped	½ cup chopped green onions
4 ribs celery, chopped	

In a Dutch oven, fry meats in margarine until brown. Add onions, celery, and garlic and cook until tender. Add broth and season with Tony's Creole Seasoning. Bring to a boil, simmer for 1 hour. Add corn bread and green onions. Adjust seasoning. Yields 10 servings.

"The employees at my company say this recipe is hard to beat. It's guaranteed to be on the table at every Chachere holiday dinner."

116

CAJUN CRAWFISH CORN BREAD

2 cups corn meal
1 tablespoon salt
1 teaspoon baking soda
6 eggs
2 onions, chopped
½ cup sliced Jalapeño peppers

16 oz. shredded Cheddar cheese
⅓ cup oil
2 (15 oz.) cans cream-style corn
2 pounds crawfish tails
Cooking spray

In a large mixing bowl, combine corn meal, salt, and soda. In a medium bowl, beat eggs thoroughly. Add onions, peppers, cheese, oil, corn, and crawfish to beaten eggs. Pour into corn meal mixture and mix well. Pour into 12 x 14 inch baking dish coated with cooking spray. Bake at 375° for 55 minutes or until golden brown. Yields 12 servings.

OYSTER DRESSING

3 dozen oysters
½ loaf French bread
1 onion, chopped
2 cloves garlic, chopped
1 bell pepper, chopped

2 sprigs parsley, chopped
1 egg, beaten
Tony's Creole Seasoning
3 tablespoons oil

Drain and chop oysters, reserving their liquor. In a large bowl, crumble bread and soak in oyster liquor. Add onions, garlic, pepper, parsley, oysters, and egg; mix well. Add oil to a large skillet; bring to medium heat. Add dressing mixture; cook for 30 minutes. If too moist, add dry bread crumbs. Yields 8 servings.

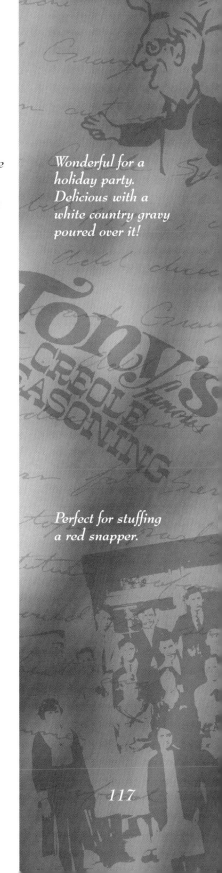

Wonderful for a holiday party. Delicious with a white country gravy poured over it!

Perfect for stuffing a red snapper.

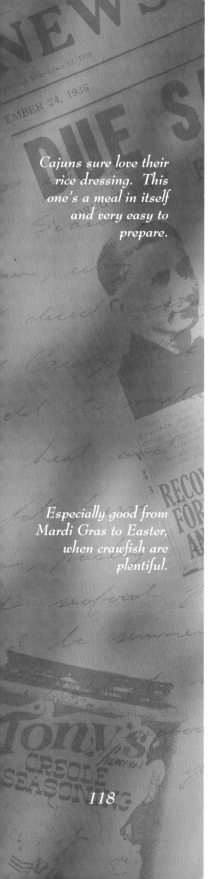

Cajuns sure love their rice dressing. This one's a meal in itself and very easy to prepare.

BAKED
RICE DRESSING

1 pound ground lean pork

1 cup rice

1 (10 ½ oz.) can onion soup

1 (10 ¾ oz.) can cream of
  mushroom soup

1 cup chopped green onions

⅓ cup finely chopped celery

¼ cup minced parsley

⅓ cup finely chopped onions

⅓ cup chopped bell pepper

Tony's Creole Seasoning

In a 2 ½ quart casserole, mix ground meat with rice. Add soups, vegetables, and Tony's Creole Seasoning. Cover with tight–fitting lid in order to retain moisture. Bake at 325° for 1 ½ hours. Yields 8 servings.

Especially good from Mardi Gras to Easter, when crawfish are plentiful.

TONY'S
CRAWFISH CASSEROLE

1 pound crawfish tails

Tony's Creole Seasoning

4 tablespoons margarine

1 cup celery, chopped

⅓ cup chopped bell pepper

3 cloves garlic, minced

½ cup chopped green onions

1 ½ cups chopped onions

2 cups steamed rice

3 slices bread (wet, wring, and
  tear apart)

1 (10 ¾ oz.) can cream of
  mushroom soup

Cooking spray

1 cup bread crumbs

Season crawfish with Tony's Creole Seasoning. Melt margarine in an aluminum Dutch oven and sauté crawfish for 5 minutes. Remove crawfish. Add all vegetables and sauté for 10 minutes. Add all other ingredients, except bread crumbs. Place in casserole coated with cooking spray. Cover with bread crumbs and bake at 375° for 30 minutes. Yields 8 servings.

CRAWFISH PIROGUES

6 potatoes
1/4 cup chopped purple onions
1 cup sour cream
2 cups shredded Cheddar cheese
1/4 cup bacon bits

2 pounds crawfish tails
1/2 cup margarine
Tony's Creole Seasoning
1/2 cup chopped green onions

Bake potatoes whole. Remove from oven; cut in half lengthwise and let cool. Scoop out center of potatoes and place in large microwaveable bowl. Reserve potato skins. Mix in all other ingredients with potato pulp except for 1/2 cup of cheese. Cook mixture in microwave for 4 minutes on high. Fill potato skins with mixture. Place potatoes in oblong baking dish; sprinkle cheese and seasoning on top and bake 30 minutes at 375°. Garnish with green onions. Yields 12 stuffed halves.

SHRIMP AND CORN SOUP

1/4 cup oil
1/4 cup all-purpose flour
1 onion, chopped
3 cloves garlic, chopped
1 bell pepper, chopped
2 ribs celery, chopped
2 (14 1/4 oz.) cans stewed tomatoes

1 (15 oz.) can cream-style corn
1 (16 oz.) bag frozen corn
1 gallon water
2 pounds shrimp, peeled
Tony's Creole Seasoning

In a large pot, make a light roux by stirring oil into flour over medium heat. Remove from heat and add onion, garlic, bell pepper, and celery. Cook until sizzling ceases. Return to medium heat. Add the tomatoes; cook 10 minutes, stirring constantly. Add corn and water. Reduce heat and simmer 1 hour. Bring to a boil and add shrimp; cook 20 minutes. Season with Tony's Creole Seasoning and serve. Yields 12 servings.

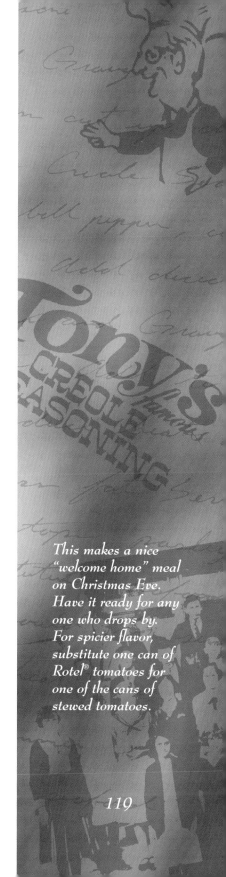

This makes a nice "welcome home" meal on Christmas Eve. Have it ready for any one who drops by. For spicier flavor, substitute one can of Rotel® tomatoes for one of the cans of stewed tomatoes.

119

This one dates way back to my childhood, made with yams from our own garden.

HOLIDAY YAM CASSEROLE

1 (16 oz.) can sweet potatoes
2 eggs
1 teaspoon vanilla extract
4 tablespoons margarine

1 (5 oz.) can evaporated milk
1 ¼ cups sugar
½ teaspoon cinnamon

In a bowl, mash potatoes and mix with all other ingredients. Place in greased casserole and bake at 400° for 15 minutes. Remove from oven and prepare topping.

Topping

1 cup crushed corn flakes
½ cup chopped pecans

4 tablespoons margarine
½ cup shredded coconut

In a bowl, mix all ingredients together and pour over casserole. Cover and bake 15 minutes at 400°. Yields 8 servings.

ORANGE NUT BREAD

3 cups all-purpose flour
3 teaspoons baking powder
½ teaspoon salt
1 egg
¼ cup sugar

½ cup chopped nuts
1 tablespoon grated orange rind
1 cup milk
⅓ cup orange marmalade

In a large bowl, sift together flour, baking powder, and salt. Add all other ingredients. Mix until thoroughly blended. Pour into 2 loaf pans coated with cooking spray. Bake in 350° oven for 45 minutes. Yields 12 slices, each.

OATMEAL BREAD

1 ¼ cups all-purpose flour
1 teaspoon salt
1 teaspoon baking powder
1 teaspoon baking soda
1 ¼ cups oats
¾ cup sugar

1 cup applesauce
⅓ cup oil
¼ cup milk
2 eggs
Cooking spray

In a bowl, sift together the flour, salt, baking powder, and soda. Add oats and sugar. In a larger bowl, combine all the liquid ingredients and blend well. Fold the dry mixture into the liquid mixture and blend well. Pour into loaf pan coated with cooking spray and bake for 1 hour in 350° oven. Yields 12 slices.

SWEET POTATO PECAN BISCUITS

2 ¾ cups all-purpose flour
4 teaspoons baking powder
1 ¼ teaspoons salt
½ teaspoon cinnamon
½ teaspoon nutmeg
¾ cup chopped pecans

2 cups cooked, sweet potatoes
¾ cup sugar
4 tablespoons margarine, melted
1 teaspoon vanilla extract
Cooking spray

In a large bowl, combine first six ingredients. In another bowl, mash sweet potatoes and add sugar, margarine, and vanilla. Add to flour mixture and mix well. Knead slightly on floured surface, then roll dough to ½ inch thickness. Cut biscuits with a glass and place on a baking sheet coated with cooking spray. Bake at 450° for 12 minutes or until golden brown. Yields 2 dozen biscuits.

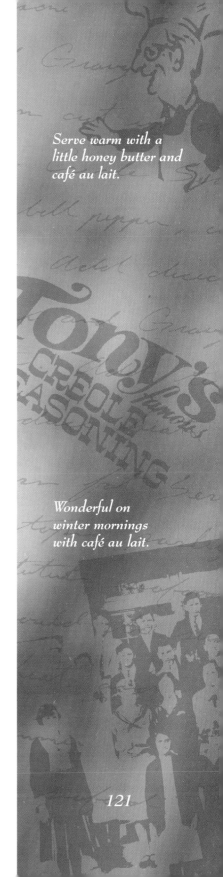

Serve warm with a little honey butter and café au lait.

Wonderful on winter mornings with café au lait.

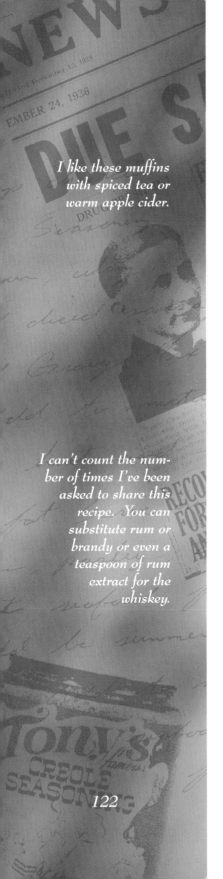

JEANNINE'S PUMPKIN MUFFINS

1 cup raisins	*4 eggs*
1 cup chopped nuts	*3 cups self-rising flour*
1½ cups oil	*1 teaspoon cinnamon*
2 cups sugar	*1 cup mashed pumpkin*

In a colander rinse raisins and nuts in boiling water. In a large bowl, mix all ingredients together and bake in muffin tins coated with cooking spray at 350° for 15 to 20 minutes. Yields 24 muffins.

BREAD PUDDING WITH WHISKEY SAUCE

3 cups milk	*2 eggs, slightly beaten*
4 cups coarse bread	*¼ teaspoon salt*
¼ cup melted butter	*½ cup raisins*
½ cup sugar	*1 teaspoon cinnamon*

In a large bowl, tear bread into small chunks. For best results use stale bread. In a saucepan, scald milk and pour over bread. Cool and add remaining ingredients, mixing well. Pour into a 1½ quart casserole coated with cooking spray. Place dish in a pan of hot water (1 inch deep) and bake at 350° for 1 hour, or until a table knife inserted into pudding comes out clean. Yields 8 servings.

Whiskey Sauce

8 tablespoons margarine	*1 egg*
1 cup sugar	*¼ cup whiskey*

Cook margarine and sugar together in a double boiler until mixture is hot and thick and sugar is dissolved. Remove from heat. Add egg and beat. Cool slightly and add whiskey. Serve over pudding.

CHERRY BERRIES
ON A CLOUD

6 egg whites

1/4 teaspoon cream of tartar

1 teaspoon vanilla extract

1 1/2 cups sugar

2 (3 oz.) packages cream cheese

1 cup sugar

2 cups whipping cream

2 cups mini marshmallows

1 (20 oz.) can cherry pie filling

1 teaspoon lemon juice

2 cups sliced strawberries

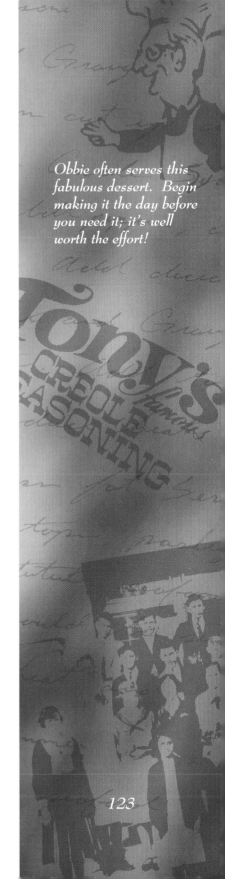

Obbie often serves this fabulous dessert. Begin making it the day before you need it; it's well worth the effort!

Meringue

In a bowl, beat egg whites with cream of tartar and vanilla. Slowly add 1 1/2 cups sugar. Beat until stiff and glossy. Bake in greased 13 x 9 x 2 inch pan for 1 hour at 275°. Turn off oven, leave in 12 hours. Do not open oven door.

Filling

In a bowl, combine softened cream cheese with 1 cup sugar. Fold in whipping cream and add marshmallows. Spread on dry meringue and refrigerate 12 hours.

Topping

In a bowl, mix cherry pie filling, lemon juice, and strawberries. Spread over filling and chill.

Cut into 12 square portions. Garnish with a sprig of mint. Yields 12 servings.

When you grow up in south Louisiana, you like sauce on everything. Here's my favorite cheesecake with praline sauce.

PRALINE CHEESE CAKE

1/4 cup margarine, melted

1 cup chopped pecans

1 1/2 cups finely crushed graham crackers

1/2 cup sugar

2 (8 oz.) packages cream cheese, softened

1 cup brown sugar

1 tablespoon all-purpose flour

1 teaspoon vanilla extract

4 tablespoons milk

3 eggs

2 dozen caramels

1 tablespoon margarine

In a bowl, mix together margarine, pecans, half of the graham crackers, and half of the sugar. Press mixture evenly into the bottom and about 1 inch up the sides of a 9 inch spring–form pan. Place pan on a baking sheet.

In a large bowl, mix together cream cheese, remaining sugar, and brown sugar. Beat with mixer until smooth. Add flour, vanilla, milk, and eggs. Beat again until smooth. Do not over–mix. Pour into unbaked crust.

Bake in a 350° oven for 40 minutes. Cool on wire rack for 5 minutes, then loosen sides of pan. Continue to cool 30 minutes. Resnap sides of pan and chill at least 6 hours.

Prior to serving, melt caramels and margarine in double boiler. Stir until smooth. Remove sides of pan and place cake on platter. Drizzle caramel sauce over cake and garnish with pecans. Yields 12 servings.

BOILED CUSTARD

1 quart milk
4 egg yolks, beaten
1/2 cup sugar

2 tablespoons all-purpose flour
1 teaspoon vanilla extract

In a 2 quart saucepan, scald milk. In another saucepan, combine yolks, sugar, flour, and 1 cup of hot milk. Mix well. Slowly add remaining milk and stir constantly over medium heat until thickened. Chill overnight. Yields 8 servings.

TONY'S CREOLE FLAN

1 cup cream
1 cup milk
1 teaspoon vanilla extract
3 eggs

2 egg yolks
1 cup sugar
1/4 cup water
6 teaspoons crushed almonds

Scald cream and milk in a medium saucepan. Remove from heat and add vanilla; stir. In a large bowl, combine eggs, egg yolks, and 1/2 cup sugar; beat until well blended. Gradually pour milk mixture into egg mixture, stirring constantly.

In a heavy skillet, heat remaining sugar over moderate heat until melted. Gradually add water and boil until well blended and brown. Pour this caramel equally into 6 custard cups. Sprinkle 1 teaspoon crushed almonds into each cup. When it sets, pour custard into cups and place in an oblong pan of hot water. Bake in a 350° oven for 45 minutes or until knife inserted in center comes out clean. Cool and unmold onto serving dishes. Serve with whipped cream. Yields 6 servings.

When I was a child, we always had this on Christmas Day served in a tall glass topped with whipped cream and a cherry on top.

Use this recipe to make Trifle.

You may use a tube pan or a single mold to make this marvelous caramel flan.

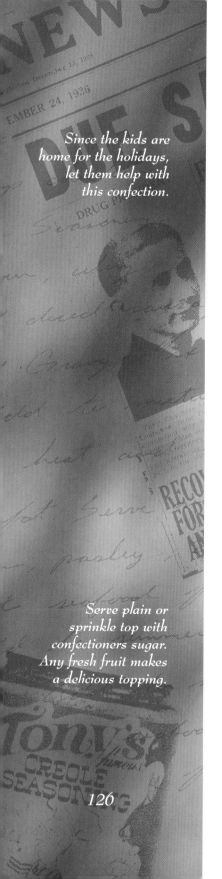

DIVINITY

5 cups sugar
1 cup light corn syrup
1/2 teaspoon salt
1 cup water
4 egg whites, at room temperature

1/2 teaspoon cream of tartar
2 teaspoons vanilla extract
1 1/2 cups finely chopped pecans

In a large saucepan over medium heat, combine sugar, corn syrup, salt, and water and bring to a boil, stirring constantly. Cook to soft-ball stage.

Meanwhile, in a large bowl, with mixer at high speed, beat egg whites and cream of tartar until stiff peaks form. Beating at high speed, slowly pour half of the syrup into the whites; continue beating while heating other half of syrup. Slowly pour hot remaining syrup into mixture; beat until mixed and very stiff. Add vanilla extract and pecans and beat until mixed. Immediately pour into a 3 quart glass dish coated with cooking spray. Cool and cut into squares. Yields 4 dozen squares.

SPICED POUND CAKE

1/2 pound butter
1 1/2 teaspoons nutmeg or mace
1/2 teaspoon salt

1 3/4 cups sugar
5 eggs
2 cups cake flour, sifted

Have all ingredients at room temperature. In a large bowl, soften butter; add spice and salt. Using a mixer beat 4 minutes. Gradually add sugar until fluffy, beating 2 minutes. Beat in 4 eggs, one at a time. Stir in all the flour at one time. Beat 2 minutes. Blend in remaining egg. Pour into well–greased, lightly floured 9 x 3 1/2 inch tube pan. Place in a cold oven. Set oven control to 300°. Bake 2 hours. Remove and cool 10 minutes; place on a wire rack to finish cooling. Yields 8 servings.

LES OREILLES DE COCHON

Pigs' Ears

2 eggs

½ cup melted butter

½ teaspoon salt

2 cups all-purpose flour, sifted

Oil for frying

In a bowl, beat eggs slightly; add butter. Add salt and flour and stir until well blended. Pinch off a small ball of dough and roll out paper thin onto waxed paper. Deep fry in 350° oil. With a wooden spoon, press down in center so that one end curls up. Fry 2 or 3 ears at a time until golden brown. Drain on absorbent paper.

Topping

1 cup pure cane syrup

½ cup chopped pecans

Pour syrup into large saucepan and cook to a soft–ball stage. Pour the hot syrup over the Pigs' Ears until coated. Sprinkle chopped nuts over ears before syrup dries. Yields 20 pigs' ears.

CREOLE FRUIT CAKE

1 cup chopped candied fruit

1 cup mincemeat

1 cup pecan halves

1 egg

1 teaspoon baking soda

1 cup all-purpose flour

1 (14 oz.) can condensed milk

In a large bowl, blend together all ingredients. Pour mixture into greased loaf pan. Bake at 350° for 1 hour for loaf, 30 minutes for mini–loaves, or 20 minutes for muffins. Double the recipe for a large Bundt ring and bake 1 hour and 20 minutes.

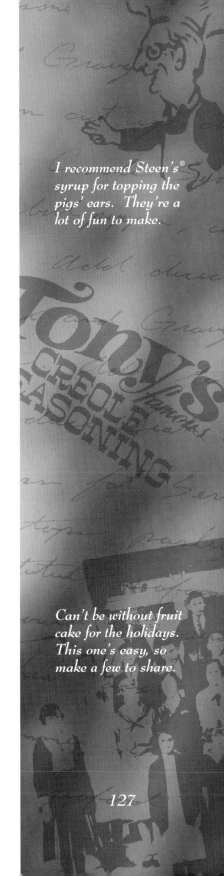

I recommend Steen's® syrup for topping the pigs' ears. They're a lot of fun to make.

Can't be without fruit cake for the holidays. This one's easy, so make a few to share.

127

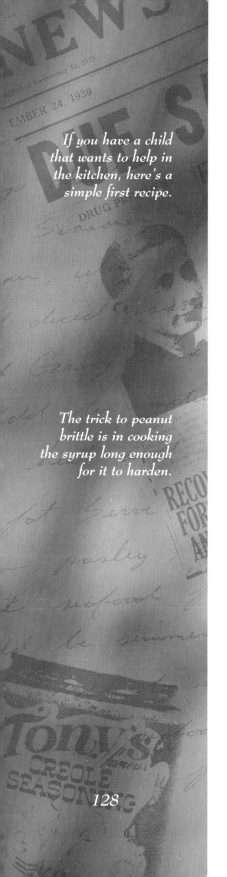

BRICKLE BARS

1 packet plain graham crackers   8 tablespoons margarine
½ cup finely chopped pecans   ½ cup sugar

Lightly grease a cookie sheet. Carefully break each cracker into 4 sections. Place crackers, side by side, in a single layer on the cookie sheet. Sprinkle pecans evenly over crackers. Mix margarine and sugar in small saucepan and boil for 2 minutes. Pour mixture slowly and evenly over crackers. Bake at 350° for 10 minutes. Remove from oven and cool. Yields 32 bars.

PEANUT BRITTLE

3 cups sugar   1½ cups white corn syrup
½ cup water   3 teaspoons baking soda
3 cups raw peanuts

In a heavy saucepan, boil all of the ingredients, except soda, until nuts crack in syrup and syrup turns yellow. Remove from heat and add soda. Stir rapidly and pour onto greased cookie sheets. When cool (about 1 hour), break into serving–size pieces. Yields about 24 pieces.

MOLASSES COOKIES

¾ cup margarine, softened
1 cup sugar
¼ cup molasses
1 egg
2 cups all-purpose flour

2 teaspoons baking soda
½ teaspoon salt
½ teaspoon ginger
½ teaspoon cinnamon
½ teaspoon ground cloves

In a large bowl, cream together margarine, sugar, molasses, and egg. In a separate bowl, sift together flour, soda, and salt. Add to liquid mixture and blend well. Add spices. Roll into balls, then roll balls in additional sugar. Place balls on sheet and press to flatten with a fork, making one horizontal and one vertical press. Bake in a 350° oven for 10 to 12 minutes. Yields 30 cookies.

CHOCOLATE OATMEAL CANDY

1½ cups sugar
½ cup brown sugar
4 tablespoons cocoa
½ cup milk
¼ cup butter, softened

½ cup peanut butter
3 cups oats
½ teaspoon salt
1 teaspoon vanilla extract

In a large saucepan, mix together sugars, cocoa, milk, and butter. Stir over medium heat until well blended. Bring to a boil and cook for 2 minutes. Remove from heat. Add peanut butter and stir until smooth. Add oats, salt, and vanilla. Mix thoroughly. Drop by tablespoonful onto waxed paper or cookie sheet and cool. Yields 24 pieces.

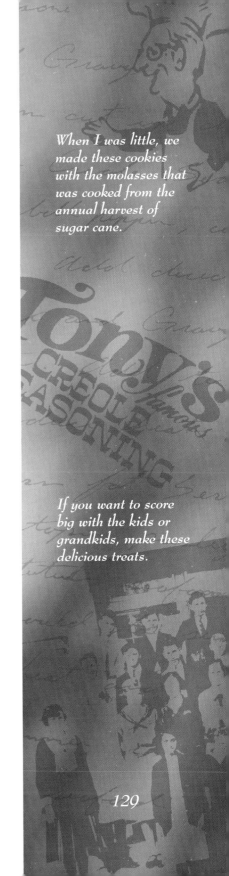

When I was little, we made these cookies with the molasses that was cooked from the annual harvest of sugar cane.

If you want to score big with the kids or grandkids, make these delicious treats.

129

BUTTERMILK CANDY

Also great made with walnuts. A dozen pieces make a nice holiday gift.

2 cups sugar
1 teaspoon baking soda
1 cup buttermilk

Dash of salt
2 tablespoons butter
2½ cups pecan halves

In a saucepan, combine first 4 ingredients and cook over high heat for 5 minutes. Add butter and pecans, stirring constantly until it reaches soft–ball stage. Remove from heat, cool a while, and whip until creamy. Drop by tablespoonful onto waxed paper. Yields 24 pieces.

FIG LOGS

Fig lovers go wild for these delicious treats.

1 cup all-purpose flour
1 teaspoon baking powder
½ teaspoon salt
1 pint fig preserves
1 cup chopped pecans

2 eggs
1 cup light brown sugar
1 teaspoon vanilla extract
Confectioners sugar
Cooking spray

In a medium bowl, sift together flour, baking powder, and salt. Add preserves and pecans. In a separate bowl, combine eggs, sugar, and vanilla. Combine mixtures into one bowl and stir. Press stiff dough into an oblong pan coated with cooking spray. Bake at 300° for 25 minutes. When cool, cut into bars and dust with confectioners sugar. Yields 12 logs.

PECAN LOGS

1 egg white

1/2 tablespoon cold water

1/2 teaspoon vanilla extract

2 cups confectioners sugar

1 cup chopped pecans

In a medium bowl, blend liquid ingredients thoroughly; add sugar gradually and mix until a fondant forms and becomes extremely stiff. Knead with hands until smooth. Shape into long rolls and cut into thirds. Roll in chopped pecans. Yields 6 logs.

CREOLE MERINGUE KISSES

3 egg whites

6 tablespoons sugar

1 teaspoon vanilla extract

2 tablespoons finely chopped pecans

In a bowl, beat egg whites until very stiff; add sugar, one tablespoon at a time, beating after each addition. Add vanilla and pecans. Cover cookie sheet with waxed paper or baking paper. Drop a tablespoon of mixture onto paper, 1 1/2 inches apart. Dry out in 250° oven until firm. This will take approximately 2 to 2 1/2 hours. Yields 36 pieces.

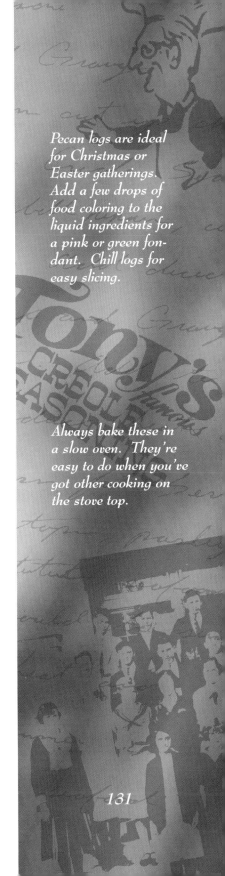

Pecan logs are ideal for Christmas or Easter gatherings. Add a few drops of food coloring to the liquid ingredients for a pink or green fondant. Chill logs for easy slicing.

Always bake these in a slow oven. They're easy to do when you've got other cooking on the stove top.

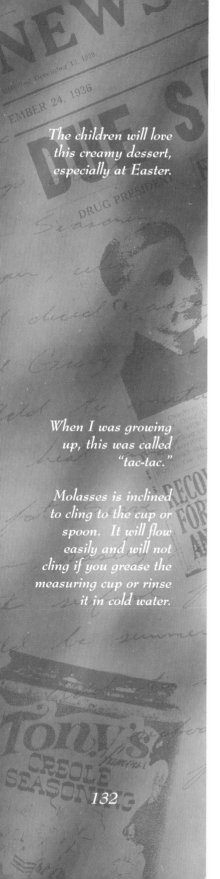

BERRY BUNNY

1 (48 oz.) strawberry soda
1 (14 oz.) can condensed milk
1 teaspoon vanilla extract

1 teaspoon almond extract
1 (12 oz.) can evaporated
   milk, chilled

In a large chilled bowl, mix soda, condensed milk, and extracts. Beat the evaporated milk in another bowl until it peaks. Pour into soda mixture and blend. Pour into paper cups and freeze until thick and slushy. Yields 24 servings.

MOLASSES POPCORN BALLS

$^1/_2$ cup molasses
$^1/_2$ cup sugar
$^1/_4$ teaspoon vinegar
$^1/_4$ cup water

$^1/_4$ teaspoon salt
1 tablespoon butter
6 cups popped popcorn

In a large saucepan, combine molasses, sugar, vinegar, water, and salt. Cook slowly without stirring until a small quantity dropped in water forms threads (hard-ball stage). Remove from heat, add butter and stir only enough to mix. Have popcorn ready in a large bowl. Pour syrup over popcorn, stirring constantly. With buttered hands, shape into balls and be quick about it! Yields 12 balls.

MRS. CHACHERE'S
HOT EGG NOG

6 cups milk

3 tablespoons corn starch

1/2 cup sugar

3 eggs

1 tablespoon vanilla extract

Pinch of salt

2 tablespoons sugar for egg
   whites

1/2 cup bourbon or rum,
   (optional)

Nutmeg

In a medium saucepan, scald milk. Remove from heat. In a
medium bowl, blend together corn starch and 1/2 cup sugar. In
another bowl, separate eggs, saving whites in a third bowl. Beat egg
yolks with a fork until lemon colored. Add yolks to sugar mixture
and blend well. Add a small amount of warm milk to egg and sugar
mixture. Stir quickly. Pour mixture very slowly into scalded milk,
stirring as it is poured in a small stream. Cook on medium heat
until it thickens, stirring constantly. When mixture coats the back
of a spoon, remove from heat. Add vanilla. Beat egg whites until
foamy. Add salt and continue beating as you sprinkle sugar into
whites. Beat until stiff. Fold egg white mixture into egg nog; add
bourbon. Pour into large punch bowl. Ladle into cups and garnish
with a dash of nutmeg. Yields 10 servings.

My wife always added
her special touch to
every occasion. It just
wouldn't be Christmas
without her Hot
Egg Nog.

"I used to go with Mama

down to the fish wagon for Friday's main course."

COMPANY'S COMING

FISH ON FRIDAY

Lent is a special time of the year to a Catholic in south Louisiana. It begins on Ash Wednesday, the day after Mardi Gras, and continues for forty days until Easter Sunday. During the forty days, we are to deny ourselves certain luxuries in reverence for the suffering of Jesus. This is known as "faire de câreme" or observing Lent.

Many Catholics give up red meats and desserts in observance of Lent. In years past, this meant lots of "couche couche" and "riz au lait" during the week and green gumbo or fish on Friday.

In Opelousas, the fish wagon would park near the downtown square on Thursdays. Everyone would go down to the square to get the fresh fish off the wagon. The peddler had fresh speckled trout, red snapper, garfish, and goo.

I used to go with Mama down to the fish wagon for Friday's main course. Sometimes it was a gar for garfish balls, sometimes a goo for sauce piquant. My favorite was her Baked Red Snapper with Oyster Dressing.

Nowadays, meat is a little cheaper and seafood is expensive, but Catholics still observe the tradition of serving seafood on Fridays during Lent. Even the local burger stands have shrimp burgers on special during Lent.

Easter weekend has evolved into a sort of homecoming for family members. Many Cajun families now have a crawfish boil or a fish fry on Easter weekend as part of their Lenten observance.

As for me, I still prefer the Red Snapper on Fridays during Lent. But no dessert.

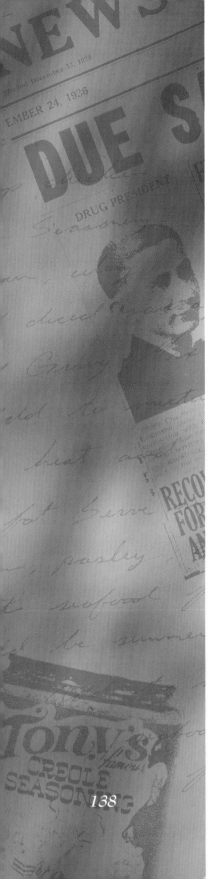

COMPANY'S COMING
Contents

MARINATED ARTICHOKE SALAD

1 bell pepper, thinly sliced
1 cucumber, thinly sliced
½ cup diced celery
1 small red onion, sliced
1 cup cubed Mozzarella cheese
1 teaspoon Tony's Creole Seasoning

1 (14 oz.) can artichoke hearts, halved
1 (14 oz.) can hearts of palm, halved
½ pound small, fresh mushrooms

Place all ingredients in a large bowl. Set aside.

Marinade

½ cup olive oil
1 tablespoon vinegar
2 tablespoons grated Parmesan cheese

¼ teaspoon minced garlic
1 tablespoon Creole mustard

Combine marinade ingredients in a small bowl; pour marinade mixture over vegetables and toss. Chill in closed container overnight. Yields 8 servings.

Serve on large lettuce leaf and garnish with crumbled bacon.

139

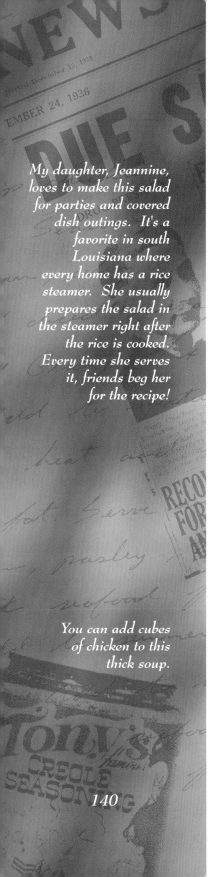

My daughter, Jeannine, loves to make this salad for parties and covered dish outings. It's a favorite in south Louisiana where every home has a rice steamer. She usually prepares the salad in the steamer right after the rice is cooked. Every time she serves it, friends beg her for the recipe!

JEANNINE'S SHRIMP SALAD

Salad

2 1/2 cups steamed rice

1 (10 oz.) package frozen peas, boiled

1 pound shrimp boiled with Tony's Creole Seasoning and peeled

3/4 cup minced onions

3/4 cup chopped celery

1/4 cup slivered almonds

Dressing

1/3 cup oil

3 tablespoons cider vinegar

1 tablespoon soy sauce

1 teaspoon Tony's Creole Seasoning

1/2 teaspoon celery seed

1/2 teaspoon curry powder

1/2 teaspoon sugar

Blend freshly steamed rice with salad ingredients in a large bowl. Toss well. Combine ingredients for dressing in a jar and shake well. Pour over salad. Serve warm. Yields 8 servings.

CHEESY CAJUN CHOWDER

You can add cubes of chicken to this thick soup.

1 cup chicken broth

3 cups water

2 carrots, sliced

1 large potato, cubed

1/2 cup corn

1/4 pound tasso, cubed

1 (4 oz.) package white American processed cheese, cubed

Tony's Creole Seasoning

In a pot, add chicken broth to water and bring to a boil. Add carrots, potato, corn, and tasso. When vegetables are tender, lower heat and add cheese. When cheese is blended into soup, add Tony's Creole Seasoning. Yields 4 servings.

CORN AND CRAB MEAT BISQUE

4 tablespoons butter
3 tablespoons all-purpose flour
1 large onion, finely chopped
1 (15 oz.) can cream–style corn
1 (10 ¾ oz.) can cream of
  potato soup
1 quart Half and Half®
½ teaspoon mace

1 pound lump crab meat
½ pound shredded Swiss cheese
1 tablespoon chopped parsley
1 tablespoon chopped
  green onions
1 tablespoon dry sherry
Tony's Creole Seasoning

In a 3 quart pot, melt butter and add flour to make a blond roux. Sauté onions until tender; add corn, soup, Half and Half®, mace, and crab meat. Bring to a boil, then reduce heat. Add cheese, parsley, green onions, and sherry. Season with Tony's Creole Seasoning. Remove from heat and serve. Yields 12 servings.

CREAM OF CRAB SOUP

¼ cup chopped onions
¼ cup margarine
3 tablespoons all-purpose flour
1 quart milk

1 (10 ¾ oz.) can chicken broth
1 pound lump crab meat
Tony's Creole Seasoning
Parsley, chopped

In a saucepan, sauté onions in margarine until transparent. Blend in flour. Add milk and broth gradually. Cook until thick, stirring constantly. Add crab meat and season with Tony's Creole Seasoning; heat. Ladle into bowls and sprinkle with parsley. Yields 6 servings.

My friend, Obbie Bordelon, prepared this delicious bisque for me. When I told her it was better than mine, she graciously lent her recipe.

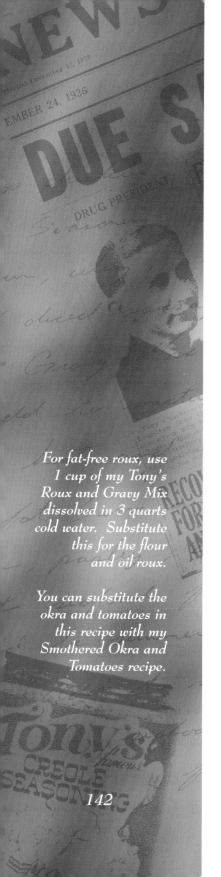

OYSTER SOUP

6 green onions, finely chopped
1 rib celery, finely chopped
8 tablespoons margarine
5 tablespoons all-purpose flour
3 dozen oysters with liquor

5 ½ cups milk
Tony's Creole Seasoning
2 cups croutons
¼ cup minced parsley

In a stock pot, sauté vegetables in margarine and flour. Drain oysters, reserving liquor. Add liquor to vegetables. Slowly add milk. Add oysters and simmer until oysters are plump and edges begin to curl. Add Tony's Creole Seasoning. Serve with croutons. Sprinkle with parsley. Yields 4 servings.

SEAFOOD GUMBO

For fat-free roux, use 1 cup of my Tony's Roux and Gravy Mix dissolved in 3 quarts cold water. Substitute this for the flour and oil roux.

You can substitute the okra and tomatoes in this recipe with my Smothered Okra and Tomatoes recipe.

1 cup all-purpose flour
1 cup oil
2 cups chopped okra
4 tablespoons margarine
1 cup chopped onions
½ cup chopped celery
½ cup chopped bell pepper
4 cloves garlic, minced
1 (14½ oz.) can stewed tomatoes

3 quarts warm water
Tony's Creole Seasoning
4 gumbo crabs, cut in half
2 pounds peeled shrimp, deveined
½ pint oysters
½ cup finely chopped green onions and parsley
Filé

In a skillet, make a dark roux with flour and oil. Remove from heat and set aside. In a large aluminum Dutch oven or stock pot, sauté okra in margarine until it is no longer stringy. Add onions, celery, bell pepper, and garlic, and sauté until tender. Add roux, tomatoes, and water to this mixture and season with Tony's Creole Seasoning. Simmer for 1 hour. Add seafood and simmer for 30 minutes. Serve in soup bowls over steamed rice, garnished with green onions, parsley, and a dash of filé. Yields 8 servings.

JUBILEE IN POINT CLEAR

During my career as a life insurance agent, I had occasion one August to visit the seaside resort community of Point Clear, Alabama. I recall on our last evening there, my wife and I had dinner in the hotel restaurant with a nice couple we had met there from Michigan. It was also their last night in town. They had been waiting for the Jubilee.

My wife and I had never heard of the Jubilee. The couple told us that it was a natural phenomenon on the beach of Point Clear. One day in late summer, scores of fin fish and shellfish rush up onto the beach. People stop what they're doing and quickly run down to the beach. There they gather as much of the free bounty as they possibly can.

That evening after dinner, our Michigan friends left Point Clear for the next destination of their trip. Had they only known it then...they missed the Jubilee by only eight hours!

We were roused from bed about 4 a.m. the next morning by a knock on our door and a gleeful voice singing, "Jubilee, Jubilee!" Pat and I threw on our clothes, grabbed the Polaroid, and hurried down to the beach to get in on the action.

Just as our friends had described, there was seafood everywhere. Crabs were crawling up on the beach. Fish swam up to the water's edge...trout, red snapper, even flounder. My wife even spotted stingrays.

Oh, man, I was like a kid in a candy store. I rushed back to the hotel and grabbed a wheelbarrow that I had seen earlier that day. We pushed the wheelbarrow down the beach and joined in the fun, choosing to confine our catch to crabs. People were everywhere, gathering up seafood all along the two miles of beach. I even saw hotel staff rolling their trousers to wade out and catch their share!

Our own plans called for leaving Point Clear the next day so we could not keep our catch. As sunrise came, we saw a family who arrived at the scene as the tide was receding and Jubilee was drawing to a close. We decided to give them our wheelbarrow full of crabs, as well as some good tips on how to cook them like us folks in Opelousas would.

To this day, I wish I still had the Polaroids we took that night when I tell friends about the Jubilee. I have a hunch where they went. I believe my wife must have sent them to our Michigan friends!

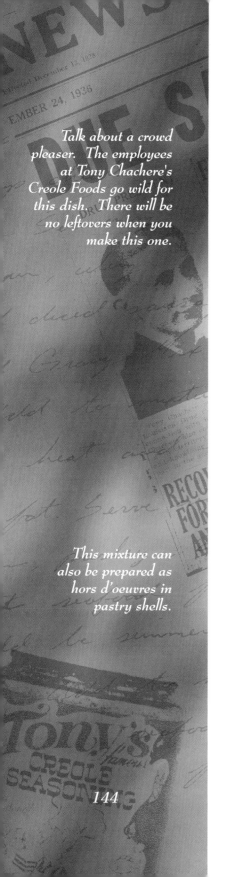

Talk about a crowd pleaser. The employees at Tony Chachere's Creole Foods go wild for this dish. There will be no leftovers when you make this one.

BLEND OF THE BAY

1 (8 oz.) package cream cheese
4 tablespoons margarine
1 onion, chopped
1 bell pepper, chopped
3 ribs celery, chopped
1 pound lump crab meat
1 pound shrimp or crawfish
1 teaspoon hot pepper sauce
Tony's Creole Seasoning

2 tablespoons butter, melted
1 (10 ¾ oz.) can cream of
   mushroom soup
1½ cups steamed rice
Cooking spray
1 cup shredded sharp
   Cheddar cheese
½ cup bread crumbs

Melt cream cheese and margarine in a double boiler. In a large saucepan, sauté onions, bell pepper, and celery until tender. Remove from heat. Stir in next seven ingredients and mix well. Place in a 2 quart casserole coated with cooking spray. Top with cheese and bread crumbs. Bake at 350° for 20 minutes or until bubbly. Yields 12 servings.

OYSTERS FLORENTINE

This mixture can also be prepared as hors d'oeuvres in pastry shells.

2 dozen oysters, shucked
2 tablespoons finely chopped
   onions
1 clove garlic, minced
3 tablespoons margarine

½ cup finely chopped,
   cooked spinach
2 tablespoons heavy cream
Tony's Creole Seasoning
6 tablespoons bread crumbs

Drain oysters and reserve liquor. Chop half of the oysters. Set all oysters aside. In a large skillet, sauté onion and garlic in 1 tablespoon margarine for 5 minutes. Add chopped oysters, spinach, cream, and Tony's Creole Seasoning. Cook over low heat for 5 minutes, stirring briskly. In a separate pot, simmer whole oysters in 1 cup oyster liquor until edges curl. Drain oysters and put 2 each in 6 ramekins. Cover with oyster–spinach mixture. Sprinkle with bread crumbs and dot with remaining margarine. Bake in a 450° oven for 15 minutes. Yields 6 servings.

TONY'S SEAFOOD BISQUE

4 tablespoons margarine

4 tablespoons all-purpose flour

1 onion, chopped

1 rib celery, chopped

2 cloves garlic, minced

¼ lemon, sliced

1 (6 oz.) can tomato paste

1 teaspoon sugar

1 pound crawfish tails

2 quarts warm water

24 fried crawfish boulettes
 (see recipe on pg. 146)

Tony's Creole Seasoning

1 tablespoon chopped green
 onions

1 tablespoon chopped parsley

Make a light roux with margarine and flour in an aluminum Dutch oven. Remove from heat and add next four ingredients. Stir until the roux stops sizzling. Add tomato paste, sugar, and crawfish. Sauté for 5 minutes. Add warm water; bring to a boil. Reduce heat and simmer for 15 minutes. Add crawfish boulettes and simmer for 15 minutes. Season with Tony's Creole Seasoning. Serve in soup bowls over steamed rice; place 4 boulettes in each bowl. Garnish with green onions and parsley. Yields 6 servings.

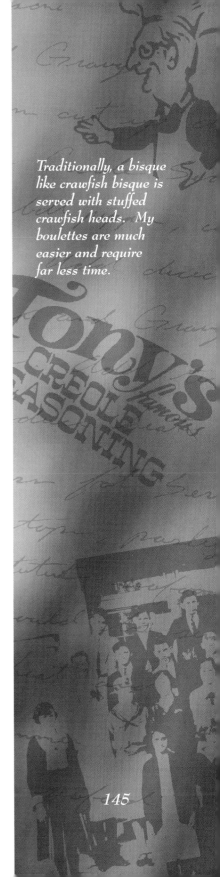

Traditionally, a bisque like crawfish bisque is served with stuffed crawfish heads. My boulettes are much easier and require far less time.

TONY'S CRAWFISH ETOUFFEE

Etouffée is the signature dish of Cajun Country. Use freshly steamed crawfish tails for excellent results.

4 tablespoons margarine
1 pound crawfish tails
Tony's Creole Seasoning
1 onion, chopped
½ bell pepper, chopped

2 cloves garlic, minced
1 teaspoon corn starch
1 tablespoon chopped
  green onions

Melt margarine in aluminum pot. Season crawfish tails generously with Tony's Creole Seasoning and sauté for 3 minutes. Remove crawfish tails and set aside. Add onions, bell pepper, and garlic to the pot. Sauté 10 minutes. Return crawfish tails to pot; dissolve 1 teaspoon corn starch in 1 cup cold water and add. Stir and simmer slowly about 20 minutes. Adjust seasoning. Serve over steamed rice and garnish with green onions. Yields 4 servings.

TONY'S CRAWFISH BOULETTES

Make these boulettes with shrimp, too. Great by themselves as an hors d'oeuvre.

1 pound crawfish tails
1 onion, chopped
1 bell pepper, chopped
2 ribs celery, chopped
2 cloves garlic, minced
2 eggs

1 tablespoon paprika
1 cup bread crumbs
Tony's Creole Seasoning
All-purpose flour
Oil for frying

Chop crawfish tails into pieces and place in a large bowl. Add vegetables. Combine mixture with eggs, paprika, and bread crumbs. Season with Tony's Creole Seasoning. If too dry, add water; if too soft, add bread crumbs. Shape in 1½ inch balls; roll in flour; deep fry in 350° oil until they float. Yields 24 boulettes.

CRAWFISH OR SHRIMP FETTUCCINE

2 onions, chopped
2 ribs celery, chopped
1 bell pepper, chopped
1 green onion, chopped
6 tablespoons margarine
2 tablespoons all-purpose flour
⅛ cup chopped parsley
2 pounds crawfish tails

2 tablespoons Jalapeño relish
½ pound Velveeta cheese, cubed
½ pint Half and Half®
3 cloves garlic, minced
Tony's Creole Seasoning
½ pound Fettuccine pasta
Cooking spray
½ cup Parmesan cheese

In a Dutch oven, sauté onions, celery, bell pepper, and green onions in margarine on medium heat until tender. Add flour, parsley, and crawfish and cook for 15 minutes. Add relish, cheese, Half and Half®, and garlic. Reduce heat and simmer for 10 minutes. Stir often to prevent sticking. Season with Tony's Creole Seasoning.

During the last 10 minutes of cooking crawfish, begin boiling the pasta so that it will be tender at the same time that the crawfish is cooked. Follow directions on the bag to boil the pasta, but do not add salt. When the pasta is tender, drain, rinse in cold water, and drain again.

In 1 or 2 casseroles, coated with cooking spray, pour some of the pasta across evenly, then cover with crawfish mixture. Continue alternating pasta and crawfish mixture until all is used up. Sprinkle top with Parmesan cheese (optional). Bake at 350° for 15 minutes. Yields 8 servings.

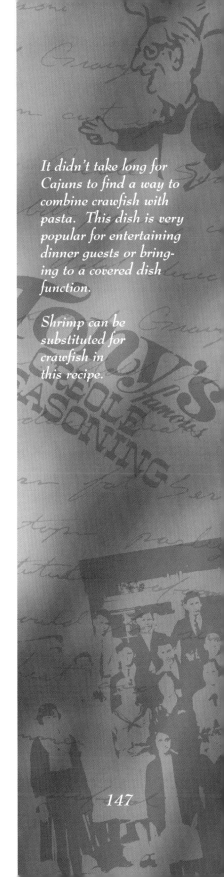

It didn't take long for Cajuns to find a way to combine crawfish with pasta. This dish is very popular for entertaining dinner guests or bringing to a covered dish function.

Shrimp can be substituted for crawfish in this recipe.

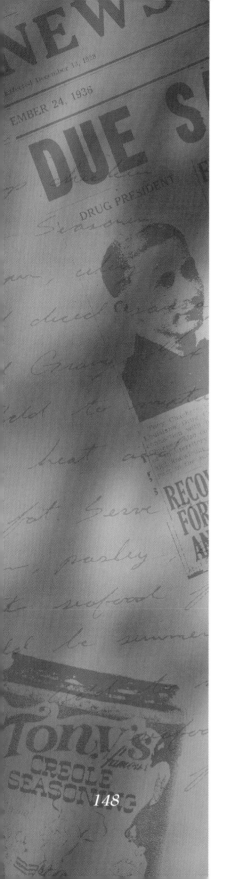

TONY'S CRAWFISH SUPREME

1 pound crawfish tails
Tony's Creole Seasoning
4 tablespoons margarine
3 tablespoons all-purpose flour
2 cups milk
4 egg yolks, slightly beaten
2 tablespoons chopped parsley

½ onion, minced
1 (3 oz.) can sliced mushrooms
1 (10 oz.) package frozen
  chopped spinach
¼ cup grated Parmesan cheese
Cooking spray

In a Dutch oven, season crawfish tails with Tony's Creole Seasoning and sauté in 2 tablespoons margarine for 5 minutes. Remove crawfish and set aside. Add remainder of margarine and flour. Stir until smooth. Gradually add milk and cook until thick, stirring constantly. Carefully add egg yolks and cook to boiling point, but do not boil. Remove from heat; adjust seasoning, if necessary. Stir in parsley, onions, and mushrooms.

In another pot, cook spinach as directed on package. Drain. Place spinach in the bottom of a 1½ quart casserole coated with cooking spray. Add crawfish and pour sauce over crawfish. Sprinkle Parmesan cheese on top of casserole. Bake at 375° for 10 minutes.
Yields 4 servings.

CRAB MEAT
AU GRATIN

8 tablespoons margarine
1 onion, chopped
2 ribs celery, chopped
4 tablespoons all-purpose flour
1 (12 oz.) can evaporated milk
1 (5 oz.) can evaporated milk

2 egg yolks
2 pounds lump crab meat
Tony's Creole Seasoning
1 cup shredded Cheddar
  cheese
Cooking spray

Melt margarine in skillet; sauté onions and celery until tender.
Add flour and blend well; add milk. Cook over low heat until thick,
stirring constantly. Remove from heat; add egg yolks, crab meat,
Tony's Creole Seasoning, and half of cheese. Transfer to square
casserole coated with cooking spray and top with remaining cheese.
Bake at 350° for 20 minutes. Yields 6 servings.

TONY'S CRAB MEAT
CASSEROLE

6 green onions with tops, chopped
4 cloves garlic, chopped
4 tablespoons chopped parsley
2 tablespoons minced bell pepper
4 tablespoons margarine
8 slices toasted bread

2 eggs
2 pounds lump crab meat
Half and Half® cream
Tony's Creole Seasoning
Cooking spray
Bread crumbs

Sauté vegetables in margarine in a pan until tender. Add crumbled
bread, well–beaten eggs, crab meat, and enough Half and Half®
cream to moisten. Remove from heat and season with Tony's Creole
Seasoning. Pour into a 1½ quart casserole coated with cooking
spray; top with bread crumbs and bake uncovered for 30 minutes at
375°. Yields 12 servings.

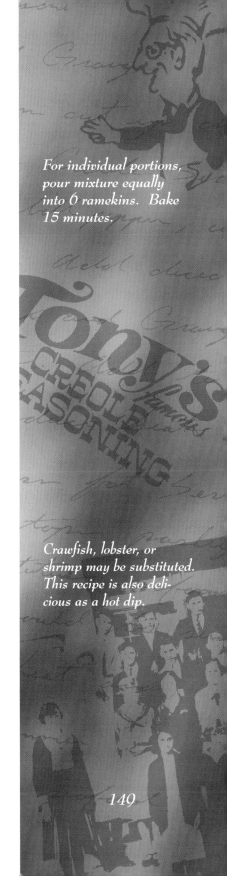

For individual portions,
pour mixture equally
into 6 ramekins. Bake
15 minutes.

Crawfish, lobster, or
shrimp may be substituted.
This recipe is also deli-
cious as a hot dip.

149

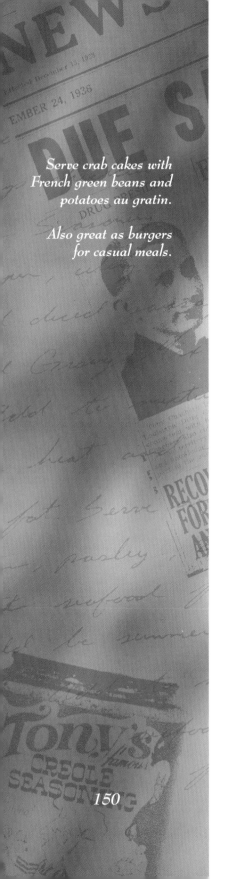

LOUISIANA CRAB CAKES

Serve crab cakes with French green beans and potatoes au gratin.

Also great as burgers for casual meals.

2 eggs
2 tablespoons mayonnaise
1 teaspoon Creole mustard
⅓ cup minced onions

1 pound claw crab meat
Tony's Creole Seasoning
1 cup bread crumbs
Oil for frying

In a large bowl, blend together eggs, mayonnaise, mustard, and onions. Beat well. Fold in crab meat, then add Tony's Creole Seasoning. Mix well. Using a tablespoon, dip out a large spoonful. Form into a round cake, then coat each side with bread crumbs.

In a heavy skillet, heat oil to 350°. Fry each crab cake until golden brown. Remove and drain on absorbent paper. Yields 8 cakes.

SHRIMP CREOLE

1 onion, chopped
½ bell pepper, chopped
2 cloves garlic, chopped
1 rib celery, chopped
4 tablespoons margarine
1 cup water

1 (8 oz.) can tomato sauce
½ teaspoon thyme
½ teaspoon crushed bay leaf
½ teaspoon basil
1 pound peeled shrimp
Tony's Creole Seasoning

In a Dutch oven, sauté vegetables in margarine for 5 minutes; add water, tomato sauce, thyme, bay leaf, and basil. Cover and simmer for 45 minutes. Add shrimp seasoned with Tony's Creole Seasoning, and cook covered for 30 minutes. If sauce is too thick, add water. Serve over steamed rice. Yields 4 servings.

CAJUN SHRIMP
STIR-FRY

4 slices bacon

2 teaspoons corn starch

½ teaspoon fish-flavored
 bouillon granules

⅓ cup water

2 pounds medium shrimp,
 peeled and deveined

Tony's Creole Seasoning

1 bell pepper, cut into
 1 inch pieces

½ cup diced celery

1 (14 oz.) can Cajun-style
 stewed tomatoes, undrained

Hot steamed rice

Cook bacon in a large wok until crisp; remove bacon, reserving
3 tablespoons drippings. Crumble bacon and set aside. In a bowl,
combine corn starch, bouillon granules, and water; set aside. Season
shrimp with Tony's Creole Seasoning.

Pour 2 tablespoons reserved bacon drippings around top of
preheated wok, coating sides; heat at medium–high (325°) for
1 minute. Add shrimp; stir–fry for 2 minutes or until shrimp turn
pink. Remove shrimp and set aside. Pour remaining 1 tablespoon
reserved drippings into wok; add bell pepper and celery and stir–fry
for 2 minutes. Add tomatoes with liquid and stir–fry for 2 minutes.
Return shrimp to wok; add corn starch mixture. Cook for 1 minute,
stirring constantly. Sprinkle with reserved bacon. Serve over rice.
Yields 4 servings.

*Makes a quick and
easy meal for dinner
guests. Use red and
yellow bell peppers for
bright color.*

For unique variations, combine your choice of any shellfish in this pie.

TONY'S
SEAFOOD PIE

1 (9 inch) pie shell
2 tablespoons margarine
1/4 cup chopped bell pepper
1/4 cup chopped green onions
1/4 cup chopped celery
1 (3 oz.) can mushrooms
1/2 pound lump crab meat
1/2 pound shrimp, boiled and peeled
1 cup shredded Cheddar cheese

1/2 cup fresh grated Parmesan cheese
1 tablespoon lemon juice
Dash of hot pepper sauce
1 egg, beaten
1/4 cup mayonnaise
Tony's Creole Seasoning
1/4 cup slivered almonds

Partially bake pie shell at 400° for 5 to 7 minutes. Remove from oven. Lower heat to 350°. Melt margarine in a large skillet and sauté bell pepper, onions, celery, and mushrooms until tender. Add crab meat, shrimp, 3/4 cup Cheddar cheese, Parmesan cheese, lemon juice, hot pepper sauce, egg, and mayonnaise, stirring well until moist. Add Tony's Creole Seasoning. Remove from heat and drain excess liquid. Spoon into pie shell and bake for about 20 minutes. Top with almonds and remaining cheese. Bake another 10 minutes. Yields 6 servings.

STUFFED FLOUNDER

2 medium-sized flounder
Tony's Creole Seasoning
1/4 cup butter
1 onion, chopped
1 bell pepper, chopped
1 cup diced celery

7 slices bread
1 cup chopped green onions,
   tops and bottoms
1/2 cup chopped parsley
1 pound lump crab meat
Juice of 1 lemon

Dehead the fish. Make a slit along the backbone from the tail to
the head. Carefully work knife into the slit and widen the pocket
the entire width of the fish, pressing sheath of knife against the
bones. The top side of the fish can now be opened like two doors.
With scissors, carefully cut away the bones from the inside of the
fish. Slide knife under the bones, loosening them from the bottom
side of the fish.

Season inside and outside of fish with Tony's Creole Seasoning.
Melt butter in skillet; add onion, bell pepper, and celery. Simmer
until tender. Soak bread in a pan of water; squeeze water from
bread. Break bread into pieces and add to skillet. Add green
onions, parsley, and crab meat. Cover skillet and cook on low heat
for 15 minutes, stirring occasionally.

Fill each flounder with stuffing; place in shallow baking pan coated
with cooking spray. Pour lemon juice over flounder, and bake in
350° oven for 30 minutes. Baste occasionally with drippings in pan.
Yields 2 servings.

*Any of my other
stuffing mixtures may
be substituted for the
bread stuffing in
this recipe.*

FLOUNDER WITH
SAUTERNE SAUCE

If you prefer, Sauterne sauce may be poured into a gravy boat and ladled over fillets at serving time.

6 flounder fillets
1 onion sliced into rings
Cooking spray
½ cup Sauterne wine
2 tablespoons lemon juice
1 bay leaf

Tony's Creole Seasoning
6 peppercorns
1 tablespoon margarine
1 tablespoon all-purpose flour
2 egg yolks

Place flounder fillets on onion rings in large, shallow baking dish coated with cooking spray. Mix wine, lemon juice, bay leaf, Tony's Creole Seasoning, and peppercorns in a small bowl and pour over fillets. Cover with a sheet of foil. Bake in 350° oven for 15 minutes.

Remove fillets from baking dish and keep warm. Strain the sauce into a cup. Add water, if needed, to yield 1 cup. Melt margarine in a small saucepan; add flour and strained sauce. Cook until thickened, stirring constantly. Beat egg yolks with 1 tablespoon water and add to sauce. Cook on medium heat for 1 minute, stirring vigorously. Return fillets to baking dish. Pour sauce over fillets. Place in 400° oven for 3 minutes. Serve immediately. Yields 6 servings.

BAKED RED SNAPPER

1 (4 lb.) red snapper
Tony's Creole Seasoning
2 tablespoons margarine
1 (8 oz.) can tomato sauce
1 teaspoon sugar

1 cup chopped onions
1/2 cup chopped bell pepper
4 cloves garlic, minced
1 cup chopped celery
1/4 cup dry white wine

Season fish, inside and out; place in open baking pan. In a saucepan, combine margarine, tomato sauce, sugar, and vegetables; cook over low heat for 30 minutes. Pour wine over red snapper, followed by the sauce. Place in 300° oven; cook for 1 hour, basting occasionally. Serve with oyster dressing. Yields 8 servings.

BAKED FISH FILLETS
IN SHRIMP SAUCE

2 pounds white fish fillets
Milk
All-purpose flour
2 tablespoons margarine
1 bell pepper, sliced
6 green onions, chopped
2 (10 3/4 oz.) cans cream of shrimp soup

1 cup boiled shrimp, deveined
1 (8 oz.) can sliced
  mushrooms, (reserve juice)
Juice of 1 lemon
1/3 cup Sherry
Tony's Creole Seasoning

Soak fish fillets in milk 2 hours in refrigerator. (Be sure that fillets have no red meat.) Remove. Dip in flour and brown lightly in margarine in a skillet. Drain on absorbent paper. Place in 2 quart casserole coated with cooking spray. In the same skillet, sauté bell pepper and onions in pan drippings until tender. In a large mixing bowl, combine bell pepper, onions, shrimp soup, shrimp, mushrooms, one-third mushroom juice, lemon juice, and Sherry. Add Tony's Creole Seasoning. Mix well. Pour over fillets. Bake uncovered at 350° for 30 minutes. Yields 6 servings.

This was my mother Nina's recipe, a Sunday and holiday favorite in the Chachere family. Stuff the red snapper with crab meat and shrimp for an even more delicious dish.

Because of my French heritage, I love cream sauces. Serve this dish with steamed zucchini and yellow squash.

155

THE LOST ART OF CAFÉ NOIR

There was a time when everyone in south Louisiana knew how to make French drip coffee. That was long before the percolator and way before Mr. Coffee. Believe me, there is no finer cup of coffee than a demi-tasse of café noir.

To brew a cup of café noir, or black coffee, is indeed an art and requires patience. When I teach someone to make it, I remember the same rules Mama taught me:

1. Start with a clean pot.
2. Always use fresh grounds.
3. Only pour in two tablespoons of water at a time.
4. Never boil the coffee.
5. Don't be in a hurry. Allow the water to drip slowly through the grounds.

Most folks kept their French drip coffee pot on the stove all day, ready to brew a little cup at any time or ready for an afternoon "visite" by friends. Passing the coffee tray around the room on Sunday afternoons was usually done by the lady of the house or the eldest daughter. The tray held freshly poured demi-tasse cups of strong black coffee along with cube sugar and sweet milk. The tray was offered to the elder guests first, then to family members, until every cup was served. An afternoon of story telling and joke sharing and news on Tante Marie's gall bladder operation accompanied the cafe noir.

Finer Creole restaurants had their own fancy twist to black coffee. Called "Cafe Brulot," it was made with sugar and spices, flamed with cognac and served after dinner. It's still served in fine New Orleans restaurants today.

Since I grew up with coffee, I'm still in the habit of drinking it all day long. Now it's brewed by Mr. Coffee, but I still only drink it a demi-tasse at a time.

TONY'S BAKED CORNISH HENS

6 Cornish hens
Tony's Creole Seasoning
½ stick margarine, sliced
½ cup basic vegetable mixture
  (pg. 25)
3 strips bacon, halved
1 cup chicken broth

1 (13 ½ oz.) can mushrooms,
  stems and pieces
½ cup chopped green onions
  and parsley
1 tablespoon all-purpose flour
2 tablespoons currant jelly

Season the hens generously with Tony's Creole Seasoning. Stuff cavity with equal parts of margarine and vegetable mixture. Place in oblong baking dish, breast side up. Top with bacon slices. Pour chicken broth in dish. Cover dish with aluminum foil and bake in 325° oven for 1 hour and 30 minutes, or until tender.

Remove foil and pour pan juices into skillet on top of stove. Return birds, uncovered, to a 500° oven. Watch closely until they are brown. Remove from oven, then cover to keep warm.

To the pan juices in skillet, add mushrooms, green onions, and parsley. Make a mixture with the mushroom juice and flour. Add mushroom mixture and currant jelly to skillet juices. Cook and stir for 5 minutes until gravy thickens.

Transfer each hen to individual plates. Pour gravy over each hen. Serve with broccoli casserole, green salad, and French bread. Yields 6 servings.

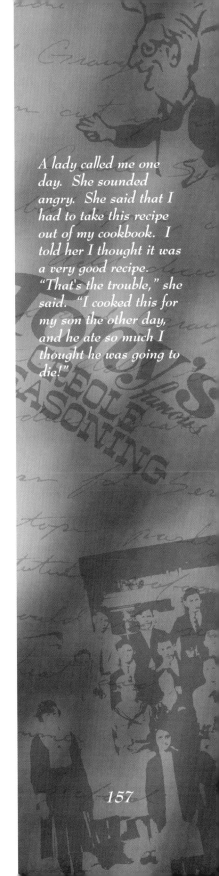

A lady called me one day. She sounded angry. She said that I had to take this recipe out of my cookbook. I told her I thought it was a very good recipe. "That's the trouble," she said. "I cooked this for my son the other day, and he ate so much I thought he was going to die!"

157

MOROCCAN CHICKEN SAUTÉ A LA TONY

2 large fryers, cut up
Tony's Creole Seasoning
Cooking spray
⅓ cup all-purpose flour
2 onions, thinly sliced

½ (6 oz.) can black olives, sliced
1 (8 oz.) can sliced mushrooms
   with juice
1 bell pepper, chopped

Season chicken with Tony's Creole Seasoning. Place in a Dutch oven coated with cooking spray. Brown a few pieces of chicken at a time. Sprinkle flour on chicken while browning. When all pieces are browned, return to the pot and add onions, olives, mushrooms, and bell pepper. Cover and cook on low heat until chicken is tender (about 30 minutes). Add water as needed to make a gravy. Serve over steamed rice with French bread. Yields 8 servings.

CHICKEN CREOLE

1 cup basic vegetable mixture
   (pg. 25)
3 tablespoons oil
3 tablespoons all-purpose flour
Tony's Creole Seasoning
¼ teaspoon paprika

1 (6 oz.) can tomato paste
2 cups chicken broth
½ cup fresh sliced mushrooms
½ cup chopped pimiento
2 cups diced cooked chicken

In a 2 quart pot, sauté vegetable mixture in oil. Stir in flour, Tony's Creole Seasoning, and paprika. Add tomato paste and chicken broth. Stir; bring to a boil. Add the remaining ingredients, except chicken; cook 45 minutes. (Add water if too thick.) Add chicken and cook for 10 minutes. Serve over steamed rice. Yields 4 servings.

VENISON
DAUBE GLACÉ

1 (10 lb.) venison hindquarter
1½ cups juice from pickled
  hot peppers
Tony's Creole Seasoning
¼ cup oil
6 onions, quartered
6 carrots, halved
2 ribs celery with leaves

4 bay leaves
Pinch of thyme
1 dozen whole cloves
4 ounces Sherry
3 (1 oz.) packages unflavored
  gelatin
4 hard–boiled eggs, sliced
2 lemons, sliced

Place roast in a large pan and pour pickled pepper juice over it.
Season with Tony's Creole Seasoning and marinate overnight or up
to 24 hours, turning once. Drain meat (retaining marinade) and
brown in oil in a large roaster. Cover meat with water. Add onions,
carrots, celery, bay leaves, thyme, cloves, and vinegar marinade.
Simmer for 4 to 5 hours or until meat is tender. Remove meat;
strain and reserve liquid.

Three pints of liquid are necessary for a 10 pound roast. If too
much, reduce by boiling down; if too little, add water. Add Sherry
to liquid; bring to a boil. Add gelatin that has been softened in a
small amount of water. Stir to blend.

Remove all fat, bone, and tendons from meat and break into large
pieces. Meat should be so tender that a knife is hardly necessary.

In the bottom of a large mold, arrange slices of hard–boiled eggs and
lemon. Place meat evenly over surface. Pour liquid gently over
meat, seal with plastic wrap and jell in the refrigerator. Any fat in
the liquid will rise to the top and can be easily removed when firm.

Turn mold over onto a large platter and decorate with parsley and
other greens. Serve with my Horseradish Sauce recipe.
Yields 12 servings.

*Any good beef roast is
just as suitable for this
wonderful old Creole
recipe.*

159

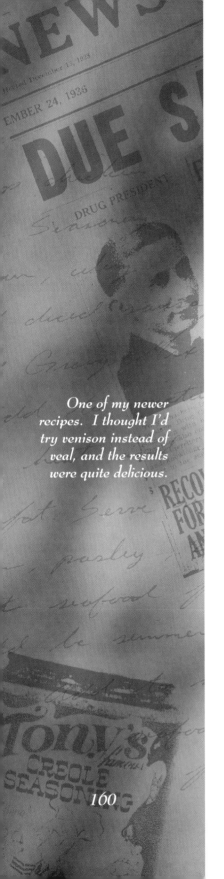

HORSERADISH SAUCE

2 tablespoons horseradish   ¼ teaspoon hot pepper sauce
1 teaspoon mustard   Tony's Creole Seasoning
1 tablespoon tarragon vinegar   ½ pint cream
1 teaspoon minced onions

In a bowl, mix horseradish and mustard. Blend in vinegar until smooth. Add onions, hot pepper sauce, Tony's Creole Seasoning, and cream. Mix well, pour into a jar, and chill.

VENISON PARMESAN

One of my newer recipes. I thought I'd try venison instead of veal, and the results were quite delicious.

1 pound venison steak,   1 onion, finely chopped
 ¼ inch thick   2 tablespoons margarine
Tony's Creole Seasoning   1 (6 oz.) can tomato paste
1 egg   2 cups hot water
⅓ cup grated Parmesan cheese   1 teaspoon salt
⅓ cup bread crumbs   ½ teaspoon marjoram
¼ cup olive oil   ½ pound Mozzarella cheese

Cut steak into 8 pieces and season with Tony's Creole Seasoning. In a bowl, beat egg with 2 teaspoons water. In another bowl, mix Parmesan cheese and bread crumbs. Dip meat in egg mixture and roll in dry mixture. Heat oil in a large skillet and fry the pieces (about 3 at a time) until golden brown on each side. Lay pieces in a shallow, wide baking dish.

In same skillet, cook onions in margarine until tender. Mix tomato paste in a bowl with hot water, salt, and marjoram. Add to skillet. Boil a few minutes, scraping all of the brown bits from the bottom. Pour most of the sauce over the steak. Top with thin slices of Mozzarella cheese; pour remaining sauce over cheese. Bake in 350° oven for 30 minutes. Yields 4 servings.

160

ROAST VENISON

1 (10 lb.) venison hindquarter
Tony's Creole Seasoning
1 bell pepper, chopped
1 onion, chopped
2 ribs celery, chopped
4 cloves garlic, minced
1 cup Burgundy wine

4 strips bacon
1 tablespoon all-purpose flour
1 (8 oz.) can mushrooms
1 tablespoon minced
  green onions
1 tablespoon minced parsley

Cut a pocket along the leg bone of the roast from the large end almost to the small end. Place roast in a large aluminum roaster. Season the roast well inside pocket, and outside with Tony's Creole Seasoning. Make a mixture of onions, celery, and garlic and fill pocket with this mixture. Close pocket with toothpicks or sew with needle and thread. Pour wine over roast and add strips of bacon on top. Cover and roast in 300° oven for 3 to 4 hours or until tender. Remove meat from the roaster. Place roaster on stove top. Add flour to the juice from the can of mushrooms and mix well. Add mushrooms, green onions, and parsley to pan juices. Cook for 5 minutes or until the gravy thickens. Slice roast and arrange on serving platter. Serve gravy over steamed rice or mashed potatoes. Yields 18 servings.

If you like your gravy sweet, add 2 tablespoons currant jelly.

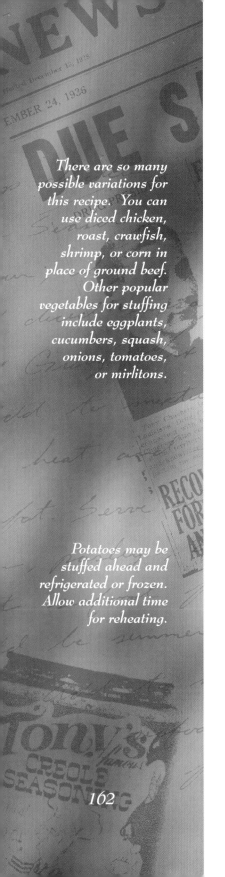

There are so many possible variations for this recipe. You can use diced chicken, roast, crawfish, shrimp, or corn in place of ground beef. Other popular vegetables for stuffing include eggplants, cucumbers, squash, onions, tomatoes, or mirlitons.

Potatoes may be stuffed ahead and refrigerated or frozen. Allow additional time for reheating.

STUFFED BELL PEPPERS

6 bell peppers
1 pound lean ground beef
1 onion, chopped
1 tablespoon margarine, melted
Tony's Creole Seasoning

1 egg, beaten
1 cup steamed rice
1 cup water or beef broth
½ cup bread crumbs

Cut peppers in half, crosswise; remove seeds and cut off stems. Set aside. In a skillet, brown beef. Drain fat. Add onions, margarine, and Tony's Creole Seasoning. Sauté until onions are tender. Remove from heat. Add egg and rice and mix well. Fill peppers with meat mixture. Place peppers in an oblong pan and pour water (or broth) around them. Top with bread crumbs. Bake in 350° oven, basting often, until tops are toasty brown. Yields 12 halves.

STUFFED BAKED POTATOES

8 baking potatoes
Cooking spray
⅓ cup margarine, softened
¼ cup chopped fresh chives

Tony's Creole Seasoning
½ cup evaporated milk
Paprika

Coat potatoes with cooking spray; prick potatoes with a fork. In a pan, bake at 400° for 1 hour or until tender. Allow potatoes to cool. Slice a small portion off the top of each potato. Scoop out pulp, leaving a thin shell. In a large bowl, mash the pulp with margarine, chives, Tony's Creole Seasoning, and enough milk to obtain desired consistency. Stuff shells with the mixture. Place on an ungreased baking sheet and sprinkle with paprika. Bake at 325° for 30 minutes or until heated through. Yields 8 servings.

EGGPLANT
PIROGUES

3 eggplants

Cut eggplants lengthwise. In a pot, parboil 5 minutes in salted water. Drain. Scoop out the pulp and set aside shells. Place pulp in a large bowl.

Stuffing

1 onion, chopped
½ bell pepper, chopped
1 tablespoon butter
Tony's Creole Seasoning
1 cup chopped ham, shrimp, chicken, or combination

½ cup steamed rice
Cooking spray
½ cup bread crumbs

In a saucepan, sauté onions and bell pepper in butter until tender. Season with Tony's Creole Seasoning. Add all ingredients (except bread crumbs) to eggplant pulp. Blend well. Place shells in a baking dish coated with cooking spray; fill shells with the mixture and top with bread crumbs. Bake in a 350° oven until shells are tender and tops are brown (about 30 minutes). Yields 6 servings.

Can be served as a light lunch main course, an appetizer, or a dinner side dish.

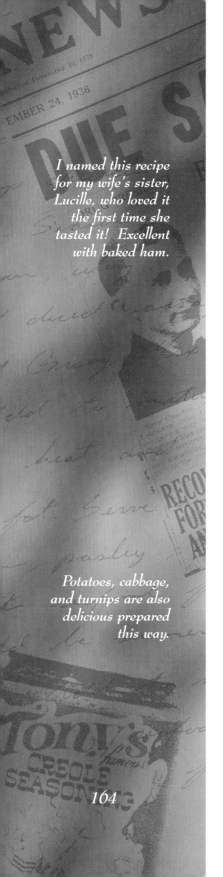

SPINACH CASSEROLE LUCILLE

2 (10 oz.) packages frozen, chopped spinach
4 tablespoons margarine
2 tablespoons all-purpose flour
2 tablespoons chopped onions
½ cup milk

Tony's Creole Seasoning
1 roll Jalapeño cheese, cubed
1 teaspoon Worcestershire sauce
½ cup bread crumbs

Cook spinach following directions on package. Drain and reserve ½ cup liquid. Melt margarine in saucepan over low heat. Add flour, stirring until blended and smooth, but not brown. Add onions and cook until tender. Pour in spinach liquid and milk slowly, stirring constantly to avoid lumps. Cook until smooth and thick. Add Tony's Creole Seasoning, cheese, and Worcestershire; stir until melted. Combine with cooked spinach. Put into a square casserole; top with bread crumbs and place in 350° oven until hot (about 20 minutes). Yields 8 servings.

CAULIFLOWER AU GRATIN

1 head cauliflower
2 tablespoons butter
3 tablespoons all-purpose flour
Milk

Cooking spray
1 cup shredded sharp Cheddar cheese
Tony's Creole Seasoning

Break cauliflower into small flowerettes. Discard the stems. In a large pot, steam slightly salted flowerettes in a steam basket over boiling water. Boil until tender (do not over cook!), drain. In a saucepan blend butter and flour. Add milk slowly, stirring constantly over low heat, until the sauce is the consistency you desire. Place the cauliflower in a square baking dish coated with cooking spray; add cheese and cream sauce seasoned with Tony's Creole Seasoning. Sprinkle more cheese over the top of the sauce. Bake at 350° until bubbly. Yields 6 servings.

AGNES KOVACH'S MIRLITON PICKLES
Vegetable Pears

12 large mirlitons, peeled and
  sliced
2 bell peppers, sliced
1/4 cup salt
12 pearl onions
1 1/2 teaspoons tumeric

3 cups white vinegar
4 pods garlic
5 cups sugar
2 tablespoons mustard seed
Salt and cayenne pepper

Place mirlitons and bell peppers in a large bowl and add salt. After 3 hours, cover with ice and keep chilled. Drain well. In a saucepan, bring onions, tumeric, vinegar, garlic, sugar, and mustard seed to a boil. Add mirlitons and bell peppers. Boil for 5 minutes. Season with salt and pepper. Pack in sterilized jars. Do not open for 4 weeks. Yields 6 pints.

TONY'S KILLER FUDGE

4 1/2 cups sugar
Pinch of salt
2 tablespoons butter
1 (12 oz.) can evaporated milk
1 (12 oz.) package semi-sweet
  chocolate bits

3 (4 oz.) bars German
  sweet baking chocolate
1 (7 oz.) jar marshmallow
  creme
2 cups chopped pecans

In a medium saucepan, mix sugar, salt, butter, and milk; heat. When it reaches a boil, allow to boil for 6 minutes. In a large bowl, combine the chocolate bits, broken up chocolate bars, and the marshmallow creme. Pour the boiling syrup over these ingredients and beat or stir until chocolate is melted and mixture is smooth. Stir in nuts and pour into a 12 x 8 x 2 inch pan coated with cooking spray. Let stand a few hours before cutting in squares. Store in container with tight–fitting lid. Yields 5 1/2 pounds of delicious candy.

In most Cajun homes, the jar of mirliton pickles enjoys a prominent spot on the kitchen table or lazy Susan. A few Jalapeño peppers can be added to the mirlitons for a twist in flavor.

Pull out this recipe when it's time for a bake sale. You'll be the first to sell out!

165

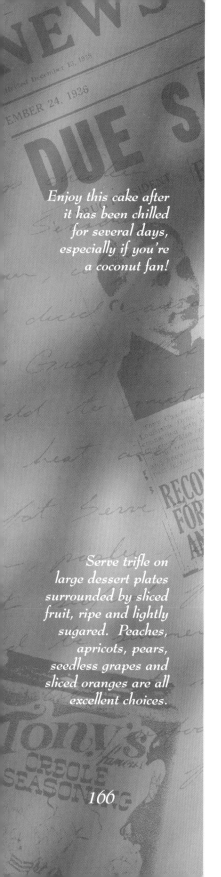

Enjoy this cake after
it has been chilled
for several days,
especially if you're
a coconut fan!

AMY VEILLON'S COCONUT SOUR CREAM CAKE

1 package butter recipe cake mix
1 cup sugar
1 (16 oz.) carton sour cream

1 (12 oz.) bag frozen coconut
1½ cups whipped topping,
  thawed

Prepare cake mix according to package directions. Make 2 layers.
After layers are baked and cooled, split each layer in 2, making
4 layers. In a bowl, combine sugar, sour cream, and coconut. Blend
well and chill for 30 minutes. Reserve 1 cup of the mixture for
frosting, spreading remaining mixture between the layers.

For frosting, add whipped topping to the remaining sour cream
mixture. Blend until smooth. Spread frosting on top and sides of
cake. Put cake in air–tight container and refrigerate for 3 days.
Then enjoy! Yields 12 servings.

TRIFLE

Serve trifle on
large dessert plates
surrounded by sliced
fruit, ripe and lightly
sugared. Peaches,
apricots, pears,
seedless grapes and
sliced oranges are all
excellent choices.

1 large sponge cake
1 large jar jam or preserves,
  any flavor

Sherry
Ripe fruit
Boiled Custard (pg. 125)

Break sponge cake into small chunks. Line the bottom of a large
bowl with a 1 inch layer of sponge cake pieces. Spread with strawberry
jam, currant jelly, or your own favorite. Cover with another layer of
sponge cake. Spread again with jam and continue until a few inches
below the top of the bowl. Pour in enough Sherry to saturate the
cake. Pour boiled custard over cake. Put bowl in refrigerator for
30 minutes. Yields 12 servings.

CHOCOLATE PIE

2 ½ cups milk

2 squares unsweetened
  baking chocolate

¾ cup sugar

½ cup all-purpose flour

3 eggs, separated

1 teaspoon vanilla extract

1 baked (9 inch) pie shell

Scald milk in a saucepan over medium heat. Add chocolate and stir constantly until melted. Add sugar and flour and cook until custard is thick. In a small bowl, beat egg yolks (reserve egg whites for meringue) and add to custard; cook 2 minutes. Remove from heat. Add vanilla. Blend and cool. Pour custard into cooled, baked pie shell and top with meringue.

Meringue

¼ teaspoon cream of tartar

3 egg whites

6 tablespoons sugar

1 teaspoon vanilla extract

In a large bowl, add cream of tartar to egg whites. Beat until peaks form. Begin adding sugar, one tablespoon at a time, and beat until stiff. Add vanilla and blend in. Top pie with meringue. Bake at 400° for 10 minutes. Yields 8 servings.

EASY MANDARIN ORANGE CAKE

1 package butter recipe
  cake mix

1 (11 oz.) can Mandarin oranges

1 (20 oz.) can crushed pineapple

1 (3.4 oz.) box instant vanilla
  pudding mix

1 large container whipped
  topping

Prepare cake mix according to package directions. When well mixed, fold in drained Mandarin oranges. Bake as directed on the cake mix box. For the filling, combine crushed pineapple, dry pudding mix, and whipped topping; chill. When layers have cooled, spread filling between each layer and ice the cake with the remaining filling. Chill before serving. Yields 12 servings.

Mrs. Chachere always made Chocolate Pie when relatives came to visit.

My daughter, Jeannine, loves to prepare this one for company.

167

"Cooks Unlimited, our supper group,
was assembled back in the winter of 1950.
The charter group was limited to 24 members."

COOKS UNLIMITED

COOKS UNLIMITED

One of Opelousas' most distinguished citizens was Henry Vincent Moseley. He had entered LSU at the age of fourteen and went on to complete his law degree at Harvard. After serving in World War I as a pilot in the Navy, Vincent settled back here in Opelousas to practice law. He was twice a candidate for governor of Louisiana. He was genteel, refined...but, deep down, one of us.

Cooks Unlimited, our supper group, was his brainchild. He assembled our group of amateur chefs back in the winter of 1950. The charter group was limited to 24 members.

The rules of the group were simple: meetings were to be held once a fortnight, every member was to bring his own liquid refreshment, new members were brought in by unanimous vote, and last, but most importantly, each member would take his turn to cook.

Vincent was quite adept at keeping our organization "ship-shape." We looked forward to his meeting notices which informed us of the menu of the upcoming meal. A sampling from our December 11, 1952 supper, with our member Veazie Pavy as chef du jour: "Avocado stuffed with Shrimp Remoulade, Patties of Oysters Bienville and Lobster Newberg, Lake Paradis Wild Duck Gumbo, Crepes Suzette, and Coffee by Anthony." Handmaidens for the evening were Moresi, Pavy, Gaiennie, Estorge, and Zoder

(the handmaidens were the fellows assigned to do the grocery shopping, vegetable chopping, prep the salad, set the tables, or generally adhere to the commands of the chef.)

When our pal Vincent died suddenly in 1958, it didn't take us long to realize that he had been the heartbeat of the group. It wasn't long after that our group informally disbanded for lack of a manager.

But what a grand nine years it was! Anyone lucky enough to have dined with us as a member or guest would declare that there were never any finer meals enjoyed in Opelousas than those prepared by Cooks Unlimited. We hosted mayors, governors, corporate "big wigs," even a Miss America. I was lucky enough to host that supper for Miss America in my home.

One of our most famous guests was Duncan Hines, the cake mix giant. His trip to Opelousas was to participate as an honored guest of our Yambilee. To host him was quite a thrill for our group and the talk of the town. However, we were usually more intent on impressing our fellow members with our abilities than any special guest. After all, fellow members were the ones who stuck around town to tout one's culinary expertise.

So, here's to you, Brother Mose. I sure miss those fortnightly suppers, the opportunity to learn, to show off, to trade stories, share heritage, and discover and modify recipes. And to enjoy one fine meal.

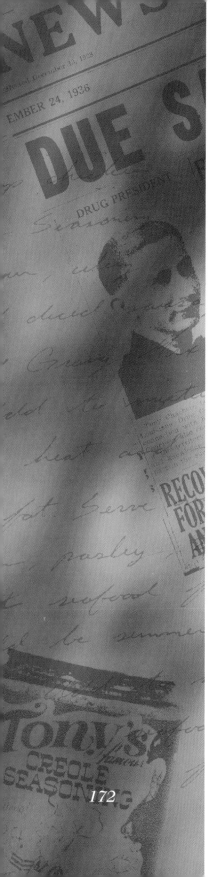

COOKS UNLIMITED
Contents

SHRIMP ARNAUD

2 tablespoons red wine vinegar
6 tablespoons olive oil
1 tablespoon paprika
4 tablespoons Creole mustard
Tony's Creole Seasoning

½ celery heart, chopped
½ onion, finely chopped
2 green onions, finely chopped
2 pound medium shrimp, boiled,
   peeled, and chilled

In a bowl, mix all ingredients together except shrimp. Serve over shrimp bedded on crisp shredded lettuce. Do not marinate shrimp in sauce. Yields 4 servings.

TURTLE SOUP

3 pounds turtle meat
4 quarts water
3 tablespoons all-purpose flour
2 tablespoons shortening
3 ribs celery, chopped
2 onions, chopped
6 pods garlic, minced
1 bell pepper, chopped

2 lemons, thinly sliced
Tony's Creole Seasoning
3 tablespoons whole allspice,
   tied in thin cloth
1 tablespoon Sherry, per serving
4 eggs, hard-boiled
Parsley

In a stock pot, boil turtle meat in water until tender. Skim foam. In a Dutch oven, make a roux using flour and shortening. Add celery, onions, garlic, and bell pepper. Remove turtle meat from the stock; strain stock; add stock to roux mixture.

Remove bones from turtle meat. Add meat to the soup, along with lemons, Tony's Creole Seasoning, and a bag of spice; simmer for 1 hour. Ladle into soup bowls. Add the Sherry to each bowl. Garnish with sliced eggs and parsley. Yields 12 servings.

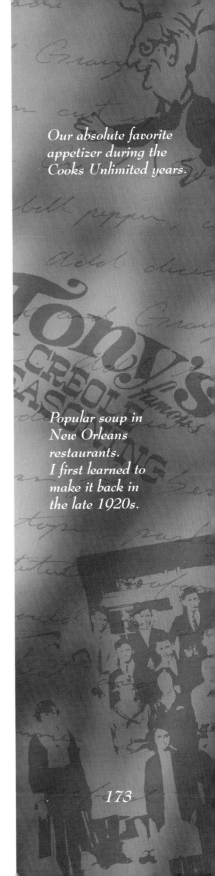

Our absolute favorite appetizer during the Cooks Unlimited years.

Popular soup in New Orleans restaurants. I first learned to make it back in the late 1920s.

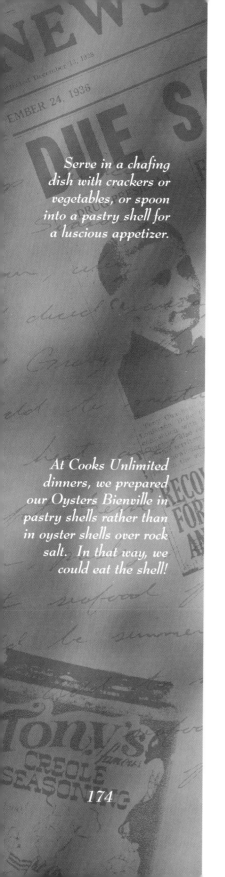

CRAB MEAT MORNAY

4 tablespoons margarine
1 bunch green onions, chopped
1/2 cup chopped parsley
2 tablespoons all-purpose flour
1 pint whipping cream

1/2 pound shredded Swiss cheese
1 tablespoon Sherry
Tony's Creole Seasoning
1 pound lump crab meat

Melt margarine in a heavy skillet over low heat. Sauté onions and
parsley. Blend in flour, cream, and cheese. Stir until cheese melts.
Add Sherry and Tony's Creole Seasoning. Fold in crab meat. Yields
12 servings.

OYSTERS BIENVILLE

8 tablespoons margarine
4 tablespoons all-purpose flour
1 pint Half and Half®
1 (4 oz.) can mushrooms
1/2 cup chopped boiled shrimp
1/4 cup chopped parsley
1/4 cup chopped onions

1/2 teaspoon thyme
1/4 cup grated Parmesan cheese
1/4 cup dry white wine
6 egg yolks
36 oysters
Tony's Creole Seasoning
6 large pastry shells, baked

Melt margarine in Dutch oven. Add flour; stir for 2 minutes.
Add cream and stir until thick. Add all other ingredients except egg
yolks and oysters. Stir well until cheese is melted. Do not overheat.
Remove from heat and slowly add beaten egg yolks, stirring
constantly. Heat oysters in their own liquor in a saucepan until edges
begin to curl. Pour off liquor and reserve. Stir oysters into mixture
and cook 5 minutes. Add oyster liquor if too thick. Season with
Tony's Creole Seasoning. Place 6 oysters in each pastry shell. Place
shells in a shallow baking pan and fill each shell with sauce. Bake in
400° oven about 10 minutes. Serve immediately. Yields 6 servings.

OYSTERS
ROCKEFELLER

6 dozen oysters (retain 3 dozen
  half-shells)
2 (12 oz.) boxes frozen spinach,
  chopped
2 cloves garlic, chopped
1/2 cup minced parsley
2 anchovies
1/2 teaspoon anise seed
1 1/2 sticks margarine

1 teaspoon hot pepper sauce
Tony's Creole Seasoning
1 teaspoon Creole mustard
Juice of 1 lemon
Bread crumbs
1 tablespoon Anisette
6 pie pans half-filled with
  rock salt
1/2 cup grated Parmesan cheese

Place oysters in a colander; drain liquor into a saucepan and add equal amount of water to oyster liquor. Cook until liquid is reduced by half. Blend vegetables, anchovies, anise seed, and oyster liquor in a blender until smooth. Combine the next 5 ingredients in the same saucepan and cook 40 minutes over medium heat. Thicken with bread crumbs as needed. Remove from heat; add Anisette.

In a 500° oven, heat shells on rock salt, 6 shells to each pie pan. Remove from oven and place 2 oysters on each shell. Cover with sauce and sprinkle with mixture of equal parts Parmesan cheese and bread crumbs. Return to oven and bake 15 minutes. Serve hot. Yields 6 servings.

HAND SALAD

On one of my turns as chef du jour at Cooks Unlimited, I decided to invite a buddy, local car salesman Harold Comeaux. Harold sold Fords in Opelousas and I leased my first Lincoln from him. Not knowing the extent of Harold's culinary ability, I recruited him as "handmaiden" and assigned him the easy job of preparing the salad greens.

Harold set out a large bowl with crispy salad fixins and invited everyone to dig in-- without plates and forks. Each hungry eater selected his favorites from the bowl, enjoying his salad by hand. Conversation was lively as the group hovered around the big bowl until the last olive disappeared.

Harold was voted in at the following meeting--hands down!

HAROLD'S HAND SALAD

2 heads lettuce
2 bunches parsley
2 bunches green onions
4 Roma tomatoes or
  3 cups ripe cherry tomatoes
2 cups small round radishes
1 (6 oz.) can ripe black olives
1 (2 oz.) jar stuffed olives with pimiento

2 (6½ oz.) jars artichoke hearts
1 (10 oz.) bottle pickled
  cauliflower
12 Italian pickled peppers
Tony's Creole Seasoning
1 (8 oz.) bottle Italian salad
  dressing

Wash vegetables in cold water and drain. Break lettuce into bite–size pieces. Chop parsley and cut green onions in 3–inch pieces. Dice tomatoes and cut radishes in half. Drain and discard juice of olives, artichokes, cauliflower, and peppers. Put all ingredients in a large salad bowl. Season with Tony's Creole Seasoning to taste; add salad dressing (enough to barely coat) and toss. Yields 12 servings.

COQ AU VIN

4 strips bacon
¼ cup margarine
2 large fryers, cut up
1 onion, chopped
3 cups red wine
1 (10½ oz.) can chicken broth

2 cloves garlic, crushed
Tony's Creole Seasoning
½ pound mushrooms, sliced
¼ cup all-purpose flour
⅓ cup water

Fry bacon in a Dutch oven. Remove bacon, crumble, and reserve. Add margarine and sauté chicken until golden brown. Remove chicken. Add onions and sauté in pan drippings until tender. Return chicken to pot; add wine, broth, garlic, and Tony's Creole Seasoning. Simmer for 30 minutes or until chicken is tender. Remove chicken from pot and place on a serving platter. To the Dutch oven, add mushrooms, crumbled bacon, and a flour and water mixture to thicken the gravy. Cook 5 minutes. Pour some of the gravy over the chicken; pour remaining gravy into a gravy boat. Yields 6 servings.

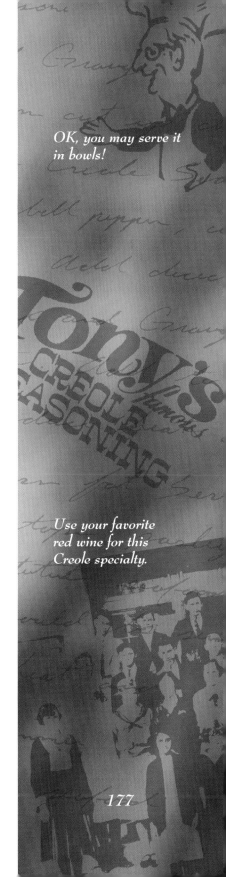

OK, you may serve it in bowls!

Use your favorite red wine for this Creole specialty.

WILD GAME
MARINADE

1 cup water
2 tablespoons vinegar
1 sliced lemon
½ dozen crushed peppercorns
½ carrot, chopped
1 rib celery, chopped
1 onion, finely chopped

1 teaspoon crushed bay leaves
¼ cup minced parsley
3 crushed cloves
Tony's Creole Seasoning
2 cloves garlic
2 tablespoons oil

In a bowl, combine all ingredients. When ready to use, pour over meat. Marinate in refrigerator overnight for all wild game—the longer the better.

VINCENT MOSELEY'S
PIGEONNEAUX EN PARADIS

6 squab
Tony's Creole Seasoning
6 tablespoons margarine
½ cup chopped onions

½ cup chopped carrots
1 cup chopped celery
2 cups Wild Game Marinade
   recipe

Season squab well, inside and out with Tony's Creole Seasoning. Rub with margarine. In a bowl, combine vegetables; add 1 tablespoon of mixture to inside of each squab and the remainder on the bottom of a deep baking pan or in a casserole. Place squab in pan and pour wild game marinade over squab; cover and bake in 350° oven for 30 minutes or until tender. Yields 6 servings.

ROAST GOOSE WITH CHOUCROUTE STUFFING

1 (8 lb.) goose
1 cup water
4 pounds sauerkraut
2 cups finely chopped onions
2 cups finely chopped apples

1 cup grated potato
1 tablespoon caraway seeds
Tony's Creole Seasoning
Thread and string

Remove all loose fat from inside goose and dice fat into ½ inch chunks. In a small covered saucepan, simmer fat with water for 20 minutes. Uncover pan and boil liquid completely away. Fat will begin to sputter. Continue to cook until it stops. Strain fat into a bowl and reserve.

Drain sauerkraut and wash well under cold running water. To reduce sourness, soak in cold water 20 minutes. Squeeze dry by the handful. Heat 6 tablespoons goose fat in a heavy 12 inch skillet; add onions and sauerkraut. Stirring occasionally, cook uncovered 10 minutes. Transfer sauerkraut mixture to a large mixing bowl. Add apples, potato, caraway seeds, and Tony's Creole Seasoning.

Wash goose inside and out with cold running water. Pat dry with absorbent paper and sprinkle cavity generously with Tony's Creole Seasoning. Fill goose with sauerkraut stuffing; sew opening and tie legs with string. Set goose, breast up, on a rack in a large roasting pan. Cook in 325° oven 25 minutes per pound.

Remove excess fat with a bulb baster. Goose is fully cooked when juice from punctured thigh runs pale yellow. Transfer goose to serving platter; cut and remove thread and string. Transfer stuffing to a serving dish; garnish with sprigs of parsley. Allow goose to set for 15 minutes before carving. Yields 8 servings.

A truly elegant entree, perfect for any special dinner occasion.

GUINEA GUMBO

Just ask any Cajun which bird makes the best gumbo. The most frequent answer would be "guinea."

Back in the days when folks raised their own livestock, everyone had guineas. They were the small spotted grey birds with little tufts on their heads. And they made a lot of noise. The meat of a guinea hen was dark, moist, and flavorful. When someone mentioned they were cooking guinea, you could be sure that every place at the table would be taken.

Guineas are rare now since people don't raise them anymore. But if someone invites me over for guinea gumbo, I'll break any plans I may have to be there!

GUINEA GUMBO

1 (3 lb.) guinea hen, cut up
Tony's Creole Seasoning
½ cup oil
4 tablespoons margarine
4 tablespoons all-purpose flour
1 onion, chopped
2 ribs celery, chopped

1 bell pepper, chopped
3 cloves garlic, finely chopped
3 quarts warm water
Green onions and parsley
  minced
Filé

Season guinea with Tony's Creole Seasoning. Fry in a Dutch oven with oil until slightly brown. Remove guinea.

Add margarine and flour to the Dutch oven, along with the drippings from the guinea, and make a brown roux. When the roux is completed, remove from heat. Add onions, celery, bell pepper, and garlic. Stir well; continue to stir until sizzling stops. Return the guinea to the pot and add warm water. Bring to a boil. Simmer for 2 hours or until meat is tender. Adjust seasoning. Skim off excess fat before serving. Serve in gumbo bowls, over steamed rice. Garnish with green onions, parsley, and a dash of filé. Yields 8 servings.

CRAWFISH STEW EMILE

4 tablespoons margarine
3 tablespoons all-purpose flour
1 onion, chopped
1 bell pepper, chopped
1 clove garlic, chopped

2 ribs celery, chopped
1 pound crawfish tails
Tony's Creole Seasoning
1 tablespoon chopped green
  onions

Make a roux with margarine and flour in an aluminum pot. When chocolate colored, remove from heat and add vegetables. Stir mixture until it stops sizzling; add crawfish, Tony's Creole Seasoning, and water to cover all ingredients. Simmer 30 minutes. Serve over steamed rice and garnish with green onions. Yields 4 servings.

Serve with steamed rice, French bread, and a green salad. A good red wine is a must!

In place of guinea you may substitute chicken, duck, doves, squirrel, or rabbit.

Some people like to add ½ pound diced, smoked pork sausage to the gumbo. I like to add a pint of fresh oysters, with the liquor, about 10 minutes before serving.

My friend, Emile Benoit from Arnaudville, never allowed anyone in the kitchen while he was cooking. He was kind enough to share this recipe because he sure wouldn't let me watch while he made it.

HUGH THISTLETHWAITE'S VEAL WITH PROSCIUTTO

1/4 cup butter
1 pound veal cutlet, cut very
   thin into 3 inch pieces
Tony's Creole Seasoning
2 tablespoons all-purpose flour
1/8 pound prosciutto ham, sliced and slivered

2 tablespoons beef broth
1 tablespoon butter
1 tablespoon chopped parsley
2 tablespoons lemon juice

Heat butter in frying pan. Season veal with Tony's Creole Seasoning. Dredge meat in flour. Place in frying pan and cook over high heat for 2 minutes on each side. Remove veal. Place prosciutto in frying pan. Cook 3 minutes. Remove and place over veal cutlets. Add broth, butter, and parsley to pan. Scrape pan well; cook 2 minutes; add lemon juice. Pour sauce over meat and serve immediately. Yields 4 servings.

POMPANO EN PAPILLOTE

4 medium pompano
1/2 lemon, sliced
1 pint water
1 (10 3/4 oz.) can cream of
   mushroom soup

1 (4 oz.) can mushrooms
1 tablespoon chopped green
   onions
1 cup small boiled shrimp
Tony's Creole Seasoning

Clean pompano and place in a skillet with lemon slices and water. Poach for 5 minutes or until tender. In a saucepan, make a sauce with mushroom soup, drained mushrooms, green onions, shrimp, and Tony's Creole Seasoning. Simmer fish in sauce for a few minutes. Place fish and sauce in oiled paper bag or aluminum foil; close like a bubble around the fish. Place in oven in an oiled pan. Bake in 350° oven for 15 minutes. Yields 6 servings.

TROUT MARGUERY

3 pounds trout fillets
Tony's Creole Seasoning
3 tablespoons olive oil
2 egg yolks, beaten
1 cup melted margarine

2 tablespoons lemon juice
1 cup chopped cooked shrimp
½ cup lump crab meat
½ cup sliced mushrooms

Season fish with Tony's Creole Seasoning in a baking pan and add olive oil. Bake in 375° oven for 30 minutes. As fish bakes, prepare the sauce.

To make sauce, place egg yolks in top of double boiler over hot (not boiling) water and gradually add melted margarine, stirring constantly until mixture thickens. Add lemon juice, shrimp, crab meat, mushrooms, and Tony's Creole Seasoning. Stir and cook for about 10 minutes to heat thoroughly. Place baked fish on a platter and cover with sauce. Yields 6 servings.

TROUT AMANDINE

4 (8 oz.) trout fillets
Tony's Creole Seasoning
½ cup all-purpose flour
⅓ cup oil

½ cup butter
½ cup slivered almonds
1 teaspoon chopped parsley
1 lemon, thinly sliced

Season trout with Tony's Creole Seasoning. Coat lightly with flour and sauté in hot oil in a skillet until trout is golden on both sides. Drain oil from skillet. Add butter and brown the almonds slightly. Pour over trout. Garnish with parsley and lemon slices.
Yields 4 servings.

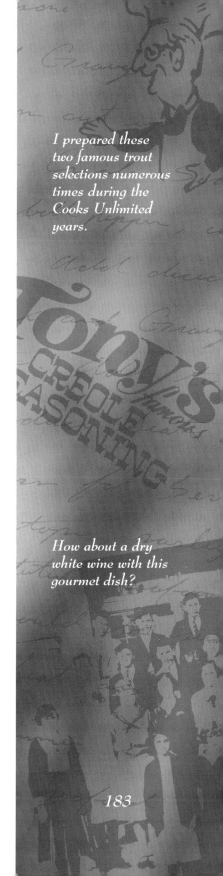

I prepared these two famous trout selections numerous times during the Cooks Unlimited years.

How about a dry white wine with this gourmet dish?

183

COQUILLE SAINT JACQUES

This is a popular dish in New Orleans. We prepared this often at our Cooks Unlimited suppers.

2 pounds scallops
5 tablespoons butter
2 cups white wine
2 tablespoons finely chopped onions
1½ cups Bechamel sauce (recipe follows)

1½ teaspoons Dijon mustard
Tony's Creole Seasoning
6 large pastry shells
1 cup bread crumbs

Combine scallops, 2 tablespoons butter, wine, and onions in a saucepan and bring to a boil. Reduce heat and simmer for 8 to 10 minutes. Remove scallops and simmer liquid until reduced to ¼ original amount. Add Bechamel sauce to liquid; add mustard and strain through a fine sieve. Slice scallops and add to sauce. Season with Tony's Creole Seasoning. Place shells in a baking pan. Heat sauce and spoon into shells. Spoon remainder of the sauce over scallops. Melt 3 tablespoons butter in a small saucepan. Sprinkle bread crumbs over tops of scallops in shells and drizzle with melted butter. Brown under broiler and serve immediately. Yields 6 servings.

BECHAMEL SAUCE

2 tablespoons butter
2 tablespoons all-purpose flour
1 cup chicken broth
1 small onion, sliced
1 small carrot, sliced

1 bay leaf
4 peppercorns
1 sprig parsley
¼ cup heavy cream
Tony's Creole Seasoning

Melt butter in saucepan and cook until frothy. Add flour, stirring constantly for 3 minutes over very low heat. In another pot, simmer chicken broth for 10 minutes with onions, carrot, bay leaf, peppercorns, and parsley. Strain broth and add to butter and flour, stirring constantly. Cook slowly until thickened. Stir in cream; cook for 5 minutes. Add Tony's Creole Seasoning. Yields 1½ cups.

EGGPLANT PARMESAN

2 tablespoons all-purpose flour
1 (1 lb.) eggplant
⅓ cup egg substitute
2 tablespoons milk
⅔ cup bread crumbs
Tony's Creole Seasoning

Cooking spray
3 cups Marinara Sauce
2 tablespoons grated
  Parmesan cheese
1 cup shredded Mozzarella
  cheese

Place flour in a large zip–top plastic bag; set aside. Peel and cut eggplant into 12 (½ inch thick) slices. Place slices in plastic bag; shake to coat. In a bowl, combine egg substitute and milk; set aside. In another bowl, combine bread crumbs and Tony's Creole Seasoning. Dip each eggplant slice into egg mixture and dredge lightly in bread crumb mixture. Place slices on a baking sheet coated with cooking spray. Bake at 400° for 12 to 14 minutes or until lightly browned. Coat a 13 x 9 x 2 inch baking dish with cooking spray. Layer half of eggplant slices in dish, overlapping slightly; spoon half of hot Marinara Sauce over eggplant. Repeat with remaining eggplant and sauce. Sprinkle with cheeses and bake 5 minutes or until cheeses melt. Yields 6 servings.

Marinara Sauce

Cooking spray
¾ cup chopped onions
½ cup coarsely grated carrots
3 cloves garlic, minced
2 (14½ oz.) cans tomatoes with Italian spices, chopped

Tony's Creole Seasoning
1 bay leaf
1½ teaspoons red wine vinegar

Coat a Dutch oven with cooking spray; place over medium–high heat until hot. Add onions, carrots, and garlic; sauté until tender. Add tomatoes and their liquid, Tony's Creole Seasoning, and bay leaf. Bring to a boil. Reduce heat and cook 30 minutes, stirring occasionally. Remove bay leaf; place sauce in blender or food processor. Blend for 5 seconds (mixture will not be smooth). Return sauce to Dutch oven; add vinegar, and cook 5 minutes. Yields 3 cups.

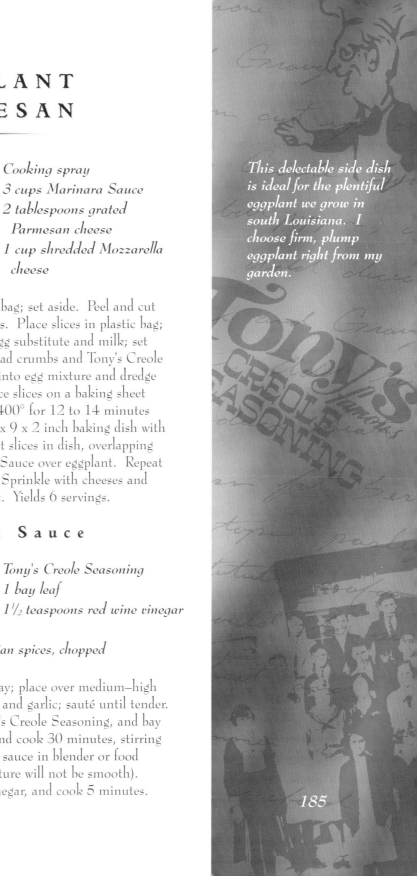

This delectable side dish is ideal for the plentiful eggplant we grow in south Louisiana. I choose firm, plump eggplant right from my garden.

185

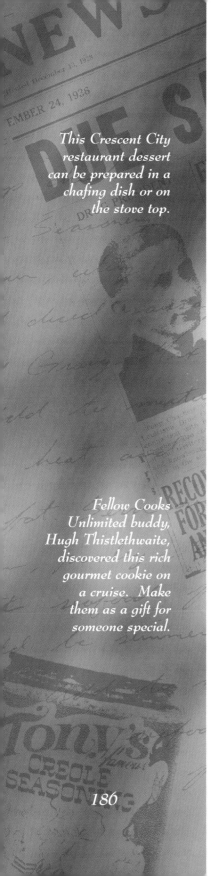

BANANAS FOSTER

1 tablespoon margarine
³/₄ cup packed brown sugar
½ teaspoon cinnamon
1 ounce banana liqueur

6 bananas, halved length–
wise and crosswise
2 ounces rum
6 scoops vanilla ice cream

Melt margarine over alcohol burner in chafing dish. Add sugar, cinnamon, and banana liqueur. Stir to mix. Heat for a few minutes, then place halved bananas in sauce. Sauté and baste lightly until bananas are soft. Add rum and allow to heat well. Ignite and allow sauce to flame until it dries out, tipping pan in a circular motion to prolong flaming. Place scoop of ice cream in each of 6 bowls. Place 4 banana pieces on each serving of ice cream, spooning hot sauce over the top. Yields 6 servings.

CLIPPER SHIP CHIPPERS

1 cup butter, softened
³/₄ cup sugar
³/₄ cup packed light brown sugar
1 tablespoon vanilla extract
1 tablespoon coffee-flavored
  liqueur
1 tablespoon hazelnut-flavored
  liqueur

2 eggs
2½ cups all-purpose flour
1 teaspoon baking soda
½ teaspoon salt
4 cups milk chocolate chips
1 cup walnut halves
½ cup pecan halves
½ cup Macadamia nuts

In a large bowl, cream butter, sugars, vanilla, and liqueurs until light and fluffy. Add eggs and beat well. In a separate bowl, combine flour, baking soda, and salt. Gradually beat into creamed mixture. Stir in chocolate chips and nuts. Mix thoroughly. Place in storage container and refrigerate overnight. Drop by teaspoonful onto ungreased cookie sheet. Bake at 325° for 10 to 13 minutes or until golden brown. Cool slightly and serve immediately. Yields 3 to 4 dozen cookies.

CHERRIES JUBILEE

1 pint jar pitted Bing cherries
1/2 teaspoon corn starch
1/4 cup water
2 ounces Kirsch®

Pour juice from cherries into the top pan or blazer of a chafing dish. Place the pan directly over the flame and bring juice to a boil. Thicken juice with corn starch dissolved in water; add cherries. Stir mixture until heated through. Pour Kirsch over cherries and ignite. Serve the flaming cherries and sauce over bowls of vanilla ice cream. Yields 6 servings.

PAT MYER'S CHOCOLATE CAKE

2 cups all-purpose flour
2 cups sugar
1 cup water
1 1/2 sticks margarine
4 tablespoons cocoa
1 teaspoon cinnamon
1/2 cup buttermilk
1 teaspoon baking soda
1 egg
2 teaspoons vanilla extract

Mix flour and sugar in a large mixing bowl. In a saucepan, bring water, margarine, and cocoa to a rapid boil. Pour over flour and sugar. Add cinnamon, buttermilk, soda, egg, and vanilla. Mix well. Pour into greased 12 x 18 inch pan and bake at 350° for 15 to 20 minutes.

Icing

1 stick margarine, softened
4 tablespoons cocoa
1 (1 lb.) box confectioners sugar
6 tablespoons milk
1 teaspoon vanilla extract
1 cup chopped pecans

Place softened margarine in a bowl; add cocoa and sugar. Mix well. Add milk, vanilla, and pecans. Spread on cake immediately after it is taken from the oven. Yields 12 servings.

We used to serve this dessert often on Ladies' Night at Cooks Unlimited. They were always impressed by the hefty amount of drama we added to flaming the cherries.

187

"My all-time favorite restaurant is gone now,
but certainly not forgotten. It was called Didee's
and was a part of the local color of Opelousas for many years."

DINING OUT

DUCK AT DIDEE'S

My all-time favorite restaurant is gone now, but certainly not forgotten. It was called Didee's (dye-dee) and was a part of the local color of Opelousas for many years.

Mr. Didee Lastrapes used to clean and cook the wild game of the local hunters as a side job. His tasty duck became so popular that he opened his own restaurant. Soon folks from far and wide came to the corner of Market and Main for his popular Opelousas Baked Duck, Shrimp and Oyster Gumbo, and Baked Chicken.

The secret of his delicious cooking was simple and has been my own method ever since I learned it from him: let the dish simmer on a low fire for a long time. The result was always the same--the meat was so tender it practically fell off the bone and melted in your mouth.

His wife Anna was quite a cook herself. Plate lunches were her specialty. Mrs. Anna's generous plate lunch was half a baked duck or chicken with petit pois, rice dressing, yams, and French bread. And she made the best oyster loaf you could ever put in your mouth. How my mother loved them! Mrs. Anna sent my mother a full loaf of a dozen select oysters every Friday, which my mother could eat by herself.

I always watched carefully as Didee and Anna cooked in their little restaurant. Countless times I watched Anna sitting in front of the oven basting chickens. And I remember every step of Didee's famous duck dish. Every time I prepare Opelousas Baked Duck, I close my eyes for a moment and I'm there again, sitting on the old cypress chair, listening to the hunters tell stories, and breathing in that distinct aroma of tender, delicious meat, gently simmering on a low fire.

DINING OUT
Contents

OPELOUSAS
BAKED DUCK

1 mature Long Island duck
Tony's Creole Seasoning
1 cup oil

1 cup water
4 tablespoons paprika
1 teaspoon chili powder

Cut duck in half and season generously with Tony's Creole Seasoning. Rub well on each side. Place duck in open baking pan and cover with a mixture of oil and water. Sprinkle generously with paprika and chili powder. Place pan in 275° oven and bake 3 to 5 hours. Baste every 30 minutes until the duck is dark, dark brown. A chicken fryer, quartered, may be baked in the same manner. Reserve pan drippings to cook another time and also to use in dirty rice. Yields 4 servings.

VEGETABLE SOUP

2 pounds cubed chuck roast
8 cups water
2 carrots, sliced
1 bell pepper, chopped
5 ribs celery, chopped

1 (14½ oz.) can crushed tomatoes
1 potato, cubed
1 teaspoon sugar
Tony's Creole Seasoning

In a stock pot, boil meat in water until tender. Remove meat from broth; add carrots, bell pepper, celery, tomatoes, potato, and sugar. Simmer until vegetables are tender. Return meat to pot and season with Tony's Creole Seasoning. Heat thoroughly and serve. Yields 12 servings.

This is a very famous Opelousas dish. The secret is in the seasoning and the long, slow basting process. It's served with dirty rice, petit pois, candied yams, a green salad, along with French bread and a demi-tasse of coffee.

*Didee Lastrapes
Didee's Restaurant
Opelousas, LA*

The Palace Café in Opelousas is most famous for its Fried Chicken Salad, the recipe for which is top secret! Chef Pete also makes this Vegetable Soup that warms your soul.

*Chef Pete Doucas
The Palace Café
Opelousas, LA*

193

CHICKEN, ANDOUILLE, AND SMOKED SAUSAGE GUMBO

Chef James Graham
Prejean's Restaurant
Carencro, LA

1½ pounds smoked sausage
1½ pounds andouille
5 pounds boneless chicken thigh
  meat, cut in 1 inch pieces
4 tablespoons oil
¼ cup butter
4 cups finely chopped onions
2 cups finely chopped celery
2 cups chopped bell pepper
¼ cup chicken-flavored granules
2 tablespoons black pepper

1¾ tablespoons red pepper
1 tablespoon garlic powder
1 bay leaf
Pinch oregano
Pinch thyme
2 teaspoons hot pepper sauce
4 (10½ oz.) cans chicken broth
6 cans water
2 cups dark roux
¼ cup chopped green onions

Warm up a large gumbo pot over medium heat, then reduce to low heat. In a cast iron skillet, sauté smoked sausage in half of the cooking oil over medium high heat until sausage begins to brown (about 4 to 5 minutes). Transfer sausage to the gumbo pot. Sauté andouille in the skillet over medium high heat until slightly browned. Transfer andouille to gumbo pot. Sauté chopped onions, celery, and bell pepper in butter in the skillet for 8 to 10 minutes.

Add all seasonings and bouillon granules to skillet and cook for 3 minutes, stirring constantly. Transfer vegetable and seasoning mixture to gumbo pot. Sauté chicken, half a batch at a time, in remaining cooking oil until slightly browned. Transfer chicken to gumbo pot. Add hot pepper sauce, chicken broth, and water to gumbo pot and bring to a boil over medium high heat. Crumble in dark roux. Bring to a boil again, then reduce heat, and cook gumbo on a low boil for 40 minutes. Simmer for 10 more minutes. Garnish with green onions and serve with potato salad.
Yields 20 servings.

STUFFED TURKEY BREAST

2 onions, chopped
1 bell pepper, chopped
3 cloves garlic, minced
4 tablespoons margarine
1/3 pound tasso, cubed

1/2 cup bread crumbs
Tony's Creole Seasoning
2 boneless turkey breast halves
Cotton string

In a skillet, sauté onions, bell pepper, and garlic in margarine until tender. Add tasso and simmer 45 minutes, adding water as needed. Remove from heat and add bread crumbs and Tony's Creole Seasoning. Refrigerate 1 hour. To open each breast half, cut a slit lengthwise so that they open completely. Stuff each half with the chilled mixture and roll. Secure by tying with string in three places. Bake at 400° for 1 hour and 15 minutes. Slice into 3/4 inch thick slices. Yields 20 slices.

CAJUN CHILI

3 pounds ground meat
1 onion, chopped
6 (4 oz.) cans tomato juice
1 (10 oz.) can Rotel tomatoes
2 tablespoons cumin

2 tablespoons chili powder
Tony's Creole Seasoning
3 tablespoons instant corn
  masa mix or corn starch

In a Dutch oven, brown meat with onions. Pour off fat. Add next 3 ingredients, and simmer 30 minutes. Add chili powder and Tony's Creole Seasoning. Adjust seasoning. Add masa to thicken. Yields 4 servings.

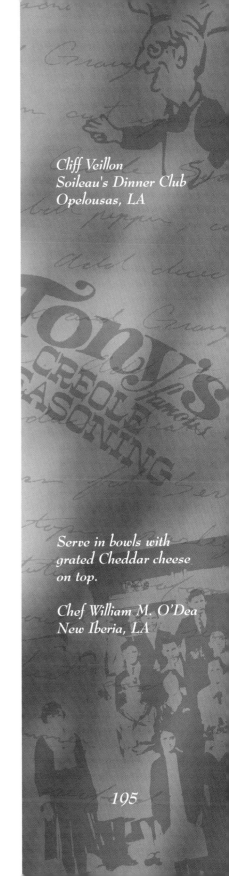

Cliff Veillon
Soileau's Dinner Club
Opelousas, LA

Serve in bowls with grated Cheddar cheese on top.

Chef William M. O'Dea
New Iberia, LA

195

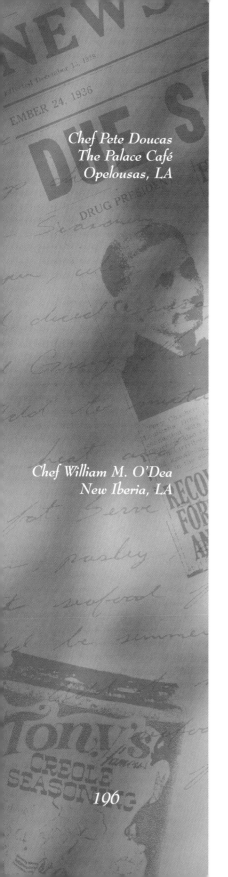

BEEF STEW

Chef Pete Doucas
The Palace Café
Opelousas, LA

2 pounds cubed chuck roast
1 onion, chopped
1 bell pepper, chopped
4 cups water

1 tablespoon corn starch
2 ribs celery, chopped
1 carrot, chopped
Tony's Creole Seasoning

In a Dutch oven, brown the meat; add onions and bell pepper. Cook until tender. Add water. In a measuring cup, dissolve corn starch in water; add to stew. Add celery and carrot; simmer vegetables until tender. Season with Tony's Creole Seasoning. Serve with boiled potatoes on the side. Yields 10 servings.

ACORN SQUASH WITH APPLE STUFFING

Chef William M. O'Dea
New Iberia, LA

1 to 2 pounds acorn or
  butternut squash
3/4 cup butter, divided
1 cup chopped onions
1/2 cup chopped celery
2 cups whole wheat bread, cubed
1/4 cup minced parsley

3 eggs, beaten
Tony's Creole Seasoning
1 cup chopped pecans
3 apples, peeled, cored,
  and diced
1/4 teaspoon cinnamon
Water

Peel squash cut in half; remove seeds, and scrape centers, reserving pulp. In a pan, melt 1/4 cup butter, and grease squash. In the same pan, melt the remaining butter, and sauté onions and celery until tender. Remove from heat; add bread, parsley, eggs, and Tony's Creole Seasoning. Add pecans, apples, and cinnamon. Add water, if necessary, to moisten. Add pulp from squash; mix well. Fill hollowed out squash, wrap in foil, and bake at 350° for 45 minutes. Cut squash in half, and serve hot. Yields 4 servings.

CATFISH OPELOUSAS

1 onion, chopped
1 tablespoon chopped garlic
8 tablespoons butter
1 pound crawfish tails
Tony's Creole Seasoning
¼ cup chopped green onions

2 tablespoons chopped parsley
1 cup water
1 tablespoon all-purpose flour
4 small catfish fillets
Cooking spray

Cliff Veillon
Soileau's Dinner Club
Opelousas, LA

Crawfish Etouffee

In a large skillet, sauté onions and garlic in butter until tender. Add crawfish tails and Tony's Creole Seasoning. Cook on high heat for 6 minutes. Add ½ of green onions, and ½ of parsley, and water. Thicken sauce with flour. Simmer for 15 minutes. Remove from heat and set aside.

Catfish

Season catfish with Tony's Creole Seasoning. Place in a skillet coated with cooking spray. Cook fillets on both sides to golden brown. Catfish is cooked when it flakes with the touch of a fork. Remove from skillet and place on a serving plate. Pour crawfish étouffée on top. Add remaining parsley and green onions.
Yields 4 servings.

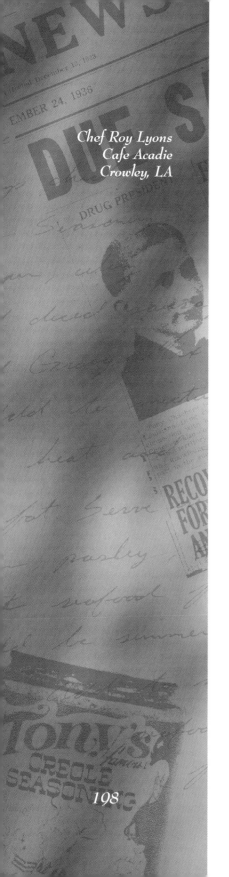

SWEET PEPPER SHRIMP

Chef Roy Lyons
Cafe Acadie
Crowley, LA

12 large shrimp, peeled and
butterflied, leaving tail
1 bottle Tiger Sauce®
4 strips bacon, each cut in 3

12 toothpicks
1 cup chopped red, yellow,
and green peppers

Wrap each shrimp with bacon and secure with a toothpick. In a plastic container, place shrimp and pour in Tiger Sauce®, enough to cover all shrimp. Marinate 12 hours. Remove shrimp from the marinade; reserve marinade.

Fire up barbecue pit, using mesquite charcoal. Line the grill with foil. Punch small holes in the foil to allow shrimp drippings to fall on the charcoal to produce smoke. Cook shrimp until golden and bacon is crisp. Pour the marinade into a small saucepan and add bell pepper. Bring to a boil. Drizzle marinade mixture over 3 shrimp on each plate and serve. Yields 4 servings.

FRIED SHRIMP

1 pound shrimp (26 to 30 count)
2 eggs
1 (5 oz.) can evaporated milk
1 tablespoon baking powder

2 tablespoons vinegar
Tony's Creole Seasoning
1 cup all-purpose flour
Oil for frying

Remove head and shell from shrimp, but leave fantail. Split shrimp down back and devein.

In a bowl, make a mixture of eggs, milk, baking powder, and vinegar. Marinate shrimp for at least 1 hour in this mixture. Remove shrimp from mixture and season lightly with Tony's Creole Seasoning. Dip in flour and deep fry in 380° oil no longer than 1½ minutes. Yields 3 to 4 servings.

SHRIMP CREOLE

1 onion, chopped
1 bell pepper, chopped
4 ribs celery, finely chopped
Oil
1 (12 oz.) can tomato paste
1 quart shrimp stock
1 tablespoon chicken base
1 tablespoon thyme

1 tablespoon sugar
1 tablespoon Worcestershire
  sauce
Tony's Creole Seasoning
1 bunch green onions, chopped
2 pounds shrimp
  (31 to 35 count)
Blond roux

Sauté onions, bell pepper, and celery in a skillet with oil until vegetables are tender. Add tomato paste and shrimp stock; cook for 30 minutes over medium heat. Add chicken base, thyme, sugar, Worcestershire sauce, Tony's Creole Seasoning, and green onions. Cook for another 15 minutes. Add shrimp and roux. Simmer for 5 minutes. Serve over steamed rice. Yields 4 servings.

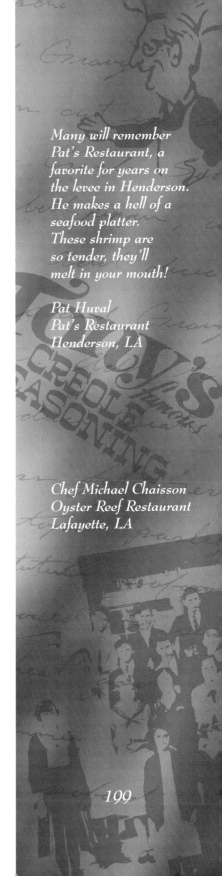

Many will remember Pat's Restaurant, a favorite for years on the levee in Henderson. He makes a hell of a seafood platter. These shrimp are so tender, they'll melt in your mouth!

Pat Huval
Pat's Restaurant
Henderson, LA

Chef Michael Chaisson
Oyster Reef Restaurant
Lafayette, LA

199

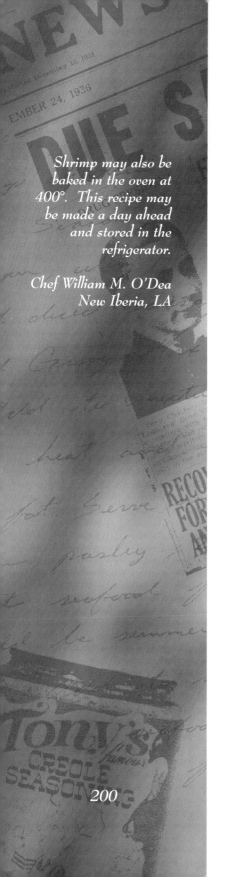

Shrimp may also be baked in the oven at 400°. This recipe may be made a day ahead and stored in the refrigerator.

Chef William M. O'Dea
New Iberia, LA

CAJUN STUFFED SHRIMP

3 pounds shrimp
1 cup olive oil
5 tablespoons lemon juice
Tony's Creole Seasoning
2 tablespoons chopped parsley
1/2 cup olive oil
1/2 cup margarine
1 cup French bread crumbs, toasted
1/4 cup grated Mozzarella cheese

1/2 cup grated Parmesan cheese
1/2 cup chopped green onions
1/2 cup chopped parsley
1/2 cup finely chopped tasso
1/2 teaspoon garlic powder
Parsley and lemon twist, for garnish

Peel shrimp, butterfly, leave on tails. In a bowl, mix marinade of olive oil, lemon juice, Tony's Creole Seasoning, and parsley. Marinate shrimp 1 hour at room temperature (or up to 24 hours in refrigerator). Remove shrimp from marinade. In another bowl, mix 1/2 cup olive oil and next 8 ingredients; stuff shrimp. Place shrimp on broiler pan and broil until browned, about 4 minutes. Garnish with parsley and lemon twist. Yields 8 servings.

CRAB MEAT IMPERIAL

¼ cup butter
2 tablespoons all-purpose flour
1 cup mushrooms, sliced
2 tablespoons pimientos
½ cup chopped celery
½ cup chopped parsley

¼ cup chopped green onions
1 pint whipping cream
⅛ teaspoon white pepper
¼ teaspoon salt
1 pound lump crab meat
Cooking spray

In a medium saucepan, melt butter; add flour blending well for
a white roux. Add all other ingredients except crab meat. Simmer
until vegetables are tender. Fold in crab meat. Pour into a casserole
dish or 4 ramekins coated with cooking spray. Bake in a 350° oven
until golden brown. Yields 4 servings.

OPELOUSAS
BARBECUED CRABS

1 cup chili powder
1 cup black pepper
⅓ cup salt
12 fresh crabs, cleaned
Oil for frying

8 tablespoons margarine
1 (14 oz.) bottle catsup
Juice of 1 lemon
1 teaspoon hot pepper sauce
Liquid smoke

In a shallow bowl, mix first three ingredients. Roll moist crabs in the
mixture. Deep fry in 375° oil until crabs float (about 7 minutes).
Remove and drain on absorbent paper. In a small saucepan, make a
sauce with melted margarine, catsup, lemon juice, hot pepper sauce,
and a few drops of liquid smoke. Pour sauce over the crabs and serve
hot. Yields 4 servings.

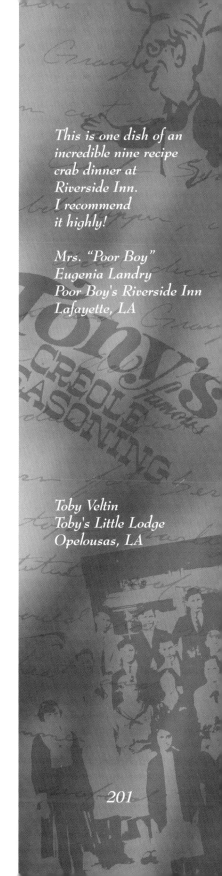

*This is one dish of an
incredible nine recipe
crab dinner at
Riverside Inn.
I recommend
it highly!*

*Mrs. "Poor Boy"
Eugenia Landry
Poor Boy's Riverside Inn
Lafayette, LA*

*Toby Veltin
Toby's Little Lodge
Opelousas, LA*

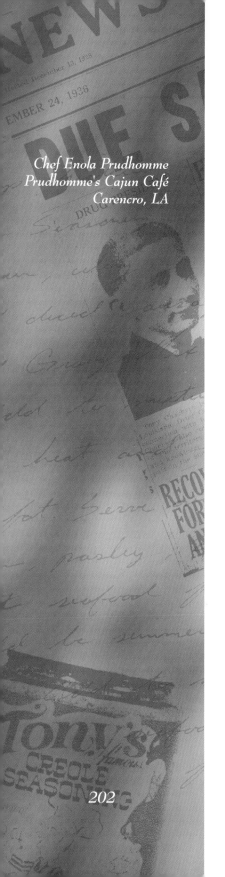

STUFFED
SOFT SHELL CRAB

Chef Enola Prudhomme
Prudhomme's Cajun Café
Carencro, LA

2 tablespoons paprika
2 tablespoons salt
1 tablespoon onion powder
2 teaspoons granulated garlic
2 teaspoons red pepper
1/2 teaspoon white pepper
1/2 teaspoon crushed oregano
  leaves
1/2 teaspoon ground thyme
1/2 teaspoon crushed dried basil
  leaves
12 fresh soft shell crabs,
  cleaned
3 tablespoons unsalted butter

1 cup finely chopped onions
1/2 cup finely chopped
  green bell pepper
1/2 cup finely chopped
  red bell pepper
1/2 cup finely chopped green onions
1/2 cup cream of mushroom soup
1/4 cup whipping cream
1 tablespoon Creole mustard
1 teaspoon yellow mustard
1 cup dry bread crumbs
2 tablespoons finely chopped
  parsley
1 pound lump crab meat

For Frying

3 quarts oil
1 (12 oz.) can evaporated milk
1/2 cup water

2 eggs
3 cups all-purpose flour

For Garlic Butter

3 tablespoons butter
2 teaspoons minced garlic

1/4 cup chopped green onions
1 pound lump crab meat

In a small bowl, combine the first 9 ingredients and mix well. Sprinkle 3 tablespoons of the seasoning mix over both sides of crabs. Reserve remaining seasoning. Place the seasoned crabs in refrigerator.

202

In a medium pot, add the butter and place over high heat. Add the onions and peppers. Cook and stir for 5 minutes. Reduce heat to medium. Stir in the green onions, mushroom soup, whipping cream, mustards, and 1 tablespoon of the reserved seasoning. Cook and stir for 2 minutes, stirring often. Remove from heat. Stir in the bread crumbs, parsley, and crab meat, being careful not to break up the crab meat. Place mixture in the refrigerator until completely cooled. Put the cooled stuffing mixture into a pastry bag with a large tip. Lift each side of the crab shell and fill each with the mixture. Return to refrigerator for 1 hour before frying.

Heat the oil to 375°. In a medium bowl, add the evaporated milk, water, and eggs; beat well. Place the flour in a large platter and sprinkle with 1 tablespoon of the reserved seasoning mix; mix well. Dredge each crab through the flour, then dip each in the egg and milk mixture, then dredge again through the flour. Drop crabs carefully into hot oil and cook until golden brown. Drain on absorbent paper; set aside and keep warm.

In a small skillet over medium heat, melt the butter. Add the garlic and green onions. Cook and stir for 2 minutes. Stir in the crab meat and the remaining ½ teaspoon seasoning mix. Remove from heat. Place the stuffed crabs on a plate and spoon equal portions of garlic butter over each crab. Yields 12 servings.

FRIED OYSTERS

1 quart oysters
2 eggs, beaten
¼ cup milk

Tony's Creole Seasoning
2 cups all-purpose flour
2 cups corn meal

Drain oysters and set them aside. In one bowl, combine eggs, milk, and seasoning. In a separate bowl, combine flour and corn meal. Roll oysters in flour mixture. Dip in egg mixture, then again in flour mixture. Deep fry in 375° oil until golden brown. Yields 6 servings.

These oysters make a fantastic loaf or poboy, or pair them with hush puppies for a great oyster dinner.

Didee Lastrapes
Didee's Restaurant
Opelousas, LA

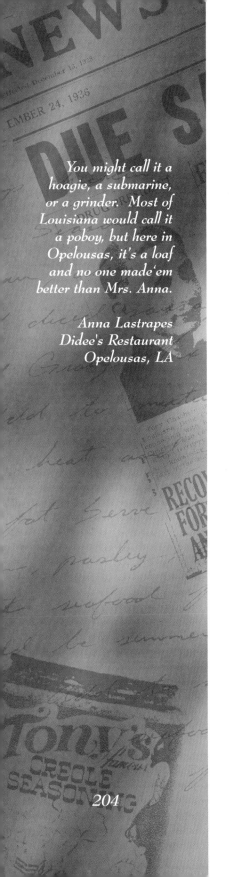

OPELOUSAS OYSTER LOAF

1 loaf French bread, unsliced	½ cup cream
Butter	1 cup bread crumbs
12 oysters	Oil for frying
1 egg	Dill pickles
Tony's Creole Seasoning	Lemon

To make a dug out with the French bread, carefully slice top one-fourth of the bread (reserve top). Scoop out insides then place dug out French bread in a 375° oven and toast about 5 minutes. Butter inside generously and keep warm.

Dry oysters on absorbent paper. In a medium bowl, beat egg with Tony's Creole Seasoning, slowly adding cream. Place oysters in egg mixture. In a separate bowl, roll oysters in bread crumbs, thoroughly covering all sides. In a skillet, fry in oil until brown; drain on absorbent paper.

Fill the hollow of the French loaf with the fried oysters. Replace top; heat in 375° oven for 3 minutes. Garnish with pickles and lemon wedges. Yields 2 servings.

CRAWFISH
PALMETTO

4 tablespoons olive oil
1/4 pound tasso
4 tablespoons each red, yellow,
  and green bell peppers
4 tablespoons diced onions
1 tablespoon Italian seasoning
4 tablespoons sliced mushrooms
1/2 cup butter

4 (2 to 3 oz.) catfish fillets
1 cup all-purpose flour
Tony's Creole Seasoning
1 teaspoon lemon juice
1 teaspoon Worcestershire sauce
1/2 cup heavy cream
1 pound crawfish tails

In a saucepan, heat oil; add tasso, peppers, onions, and Italian
seasoning. Sauté until tender. Add mushrooms and sauté for
2 minutes. Remove from heat and set aside. Dredge fish in flour
seasoned with Tony's Creole Seasoning. In a skillet, fry fish in butter
until golden brown on both sides, turning once. When done, add
lemon juice and Worcestershire sauce. Coat fish well and remove to
a warm platter. Cover and keep warm.

In the same skillet, add cream. Heat and stir well. Add crawfish and
vegetable mixture. Cook for 3 minutes. Adjust seasoning. Pour over
catfish. Garnish with parsley and green onions. Yields 4 servings.

Chef Frank Elder
Steamboat Warehouse
Washington, LA

Glossary

Acadiana (uh-kay-dee-an-uh). A 22-parish area which forms a triangle in south Louisiana, extending west to the prairies and east to the bayous; the primary settlement of the Acadians.

Andouille (ahn-doo-ee). A lean Cajun pork sausage with a spicy, smoked flavor.

Anisette (a-nee-zet). A licorice flavored cordial.

Bayou (bah-yoo). Small river.

Beignet (ban-yay). A square French doughnut, deep-fried and sprinkled with powdered sugar.

Béné (bay-nay). Sesame seed.

Bisque (bisk). A thick, creamy shellfish soup, usually made with crawfish, shrimp, or oysters.

Blackening. A method of quick cooking which requires a white hot cast-iron skillet and seasoned meat and yields a crust on each surface of the meat.

Blanc Mange (blawn-mawndge). A "white edible," a thick, milky custard.

Boeuf (buff). "Beef."

Boucherie (boo-shuh-ree). A community butchering which has its origins in leaner agricultural times. Each participant takes his turn providing the animal to be slaughtered and shares in the yield of meat.

Boudin (boo-dan). A Cajun sausage made of cooked ground pork, rice, and seasonings stuffed into a casing.

Bouilli (boo-yee). A stew made of boiled beef organ meats.

Bouillie (boo-yee). A boiled milk custard used especially for filling tartes.

Boulette (boo-let). A meatball, dumpling, or croquette.

Bourré (boo-ray). A Cajun card game which requires the loser of a hand to stuff the pot with chips.

Boursin (boor-zan). An hors d'oeuvre made from cheese and herbs, usually rolled in nuts.

Café au Lait (kah-fay-oh-lay). Coffee with steamed milk.

Cajun (kay-jun). An adaptation of the word "Cadien" used to describe the descendants of French settlers who began arriving in Louisiana in 1765 after 10 years of forced exile from their native Acadie (now Nova Scotia). Today, the term can describe anyone in south Louisiana who has become assimilated in Cajun culture.

Cajun Cuisine. The food ways of the Cajuns, typified by long, slow cooking in covered pots and adaptation of the native food sources of south Louisiana.

Cajun Trinity. Nickname for the three vegetables that are a must in Cajun/Creole cuisine: bell pepper, celery, onion.

Carême (kah-rim). The Catholic Lenten period; a solemn 40 days of fasting and repentance between Mardi Gras and Easter.

Cas-Ca-Ra (kass-ka-rah). A Cajun bean soup.

Cayenne (kah-yen). The pepper most commonly used in south Louisiana cooking; also used to make hot pepper sauces.

Chartreuse (shawr-troos). A liqueur.

Chaudin (show-dan). Stuffed pork stomach; also called Panse Bourre ("stuffed stomach").

Choucroute (shoo-kroot). Sauerkraut.

Choupique (shoo-pick). "Bowfin." A mud fish, usually eaten in leaner times and cooked in a spicy tomato gravy.

Chow Chow (chow-chow). A pickled condiment of chopped vegetables, spices, and peppers, similar to relish.

Coq au Vin (koh-kaw-van). "Rooster in wine"; a gourmet dish.

Coquille St. Jacques. A gourmet entree made with scallops.

Couche-Couche (koosh-koosh). Fried cornmeal eaten as a cereal with milk and/or cane syrup.

Courtbouillon (koo-bee-yawn). A spicy tomato-based seafood stew.

Créole (kree-yole). Originally described anyone who was born in the colony of Louisiana and their descendants.

Creole Cuisine. The food ways of the early Creole settlers of Louisiana, typified by access to and the use of peppers and spices, roux, and seasoning vegetables; developed from French, Spanish, and Afro-Caribbean influences.

Croquesignole (croke-sig-nole). The country cousin of a beignet; a flat Cajun doughnut.

Daube Glacé (dohb-glah-say). A spicy roast, "iced" (molded) with gelatin.

Débris (day-bree). Sa slowly cooked stew made from organ meats.

Demi-Tasse (deh-mee-tahs). "A half cup"; a small porcelain cup used to drink coffee.

Dutch Oven. The primary cooking pot in Cajun cuisine, usually made of heavy aluminum or cast iron and holds about 7 to 8 quarts of liquid.

Etouffée (ay-too-fay). A gravy made by smothering seasoned vegetables. The ultimate Cajun dish, usually made with seafood in a smothered vegetable sauce.

Filé (fee-lay). An exotic spice made from powdered sassafras leaves and used as garnish for gumbo.

Fricassée (free-kah-say). A stew made by browning then removing meat from the pan, making a roux with the pan drippings, then returning meat to simmer in the thick gravy.

Fromage de Tête (froh-modge-day-tet). "Head cheese." A congealed hors d'oeuvre made from the head of a pig.

Gateau de Sirop (gah-tohd-see-roh). Syrup cake; a sheet cake made from cane syrup.

Gratons (grah-tohns). "Cracklings"; crunchy snacks made by boiling or deep-frying chopped pig skin.

Green Onions. Sometimes called scallions, the green onion tops, or shoots, are used mostly for garnish in Cajun and Creole cuisine.

Grillades (gree-yahdz). Diced beef round, veal, or pork that has been marinated for a few days in vinegar. Yields a rust-colored gravy (sauce rouillée) when cooked. Traditionally served for brunch with grits.

Gumbo (gum-boh). A roux-based soup of poultry, sausage, or seafood, served over rice.

Haricot (ah-ree-koh). "Snap bean."

Huîtres (weet). "Oysters."

Hush Puppy. A ball-shaped cornmeal fritter.

Jambalaya (jum-buh-lie-yuh). A main dish usually made from rice and a combination of meats. Similar to paella.

Lagniappe (lon-yop). "Something extra"; an unexpected treat or favor.

Les Oreilles de Cochon (lay zoh-rays-day-koh-shon). "The ears of the pig." A treat made of thin dough, deep-fried and shaped like a pig's ear, then covered in syrup and chopped nuts.

Maque Chou (mock-shoo). A dish made by scraping young corn off the cob and smothering the kernels in tomatoes, onion, and spices.

Mardi Gras (mar-dee-graw). "Fat Tuesday." The final day of celebration on the Tuesday before Ash Wednesday which begins Lent.

Mirliton (mer-lee-tawn). A vegetable pear or chayote.

Pâcqué (pah-kay). An Easter game of trying to break your opponent's Easter egg using your own; the winner is the last unbroken egg.

Pain Perdu (pan-pear-doo). "Lost bread." A breakfast treat made by soaking old bread in an egg batter, then frying and topping with cane syrup or powdered sugar.

Pecan (puh-kahn). A flavorful nut primarily found in the South.

Petit Pois (puh-tee-pwah). Small green peas.

Pirogue (Pee-roh). A small, narrow boat once used primarily for marsh and bayou travel.

Poboy. A sandwich made of meats stuffed in a length of French bread.

Pomme de Terre (pawm-duh-tare). "Apple of the earth"; potato.

Pousse Café (poos-kah-fay). An after dinner drink made from liqueurs and coffee.

Praline (prah-leen). A candy usually made from cream, sugar, and pecans.

Reintier (ran-chay). "Backbone." A stew made from the meaty backbone of the hog.

Riz au Lait (ree-zoh-lay). "Rice with milk"; rice pudding.

Roux (roo). A base for gumbo or stews made of flour browned in oil.

Sauce Piquante (saws-pee-kawnt). "Spicy sauce"; a thick, spicy stew.

Sauté (saw-tay). To cook in a small amount of oil or margarine.

Tarte (tart). "Tart"; sweet dough pie.

Tasso (tah-soh). Strips of spiced pork or beef which are smoked like jerky and used to flavor many dishes; Cajun pepperoni.

Index of Recipes

C

214

W

Y

Z

June 14, 1905 - March 19, 1995

The Ole Master was taken from us on March 19, 1995.

Some say that death comes when your work on earth is complete. That may be partly true. Mr. Tony had just completed work on this book in early March and was looking forward to its publication near his 90th birthday in June.

On March 13, he received a most wonderful accolade. His peers in the American Culinary Federation honored him as the first inductee into the Louisiana Chefs Hall of Fame. What a fitting tribute to his lifetime of devotion to his favorite work.

But Mr. Tony's work was really never done. His lifetime of accomplishments can attest to that: Three successful careers, a long list of awards and citations, travel from coast to coast and abroad, a cupboard full of products bearing his name, and patriarch to a huge family of 54.

But he was always looking forward to the next goal, the next new product, the next hunting or fishing trip, the next family get-together, the next good meal.

We'll miss you, Mr. Tony. Thanks for leaving such a legacy and such wonderful memories.

Order Form

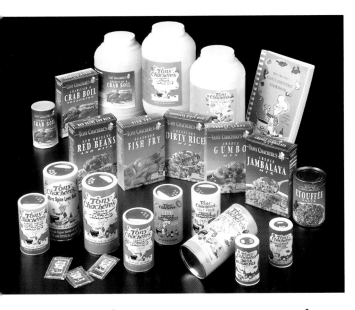

For more information, or to receive a free catalog, on Tony Chachere's delicious line of Cajun and Creole products, call us at 1-800-551-9066.

Ordering by mail:

To order additional copies of **Tony Chachere's Second Helping** cookbook, fill out the form below (or a photocopy), and mail it along with your payment to: Tony Chachere's Creole Foods of Opelousas, Inc., P.O. Box 1687, Opelousas, LA 70571.

Ordering by phone:

To order by phone, call 1-800-551-9066. Our hours are 8 a.m. to 5 p.m., Central Standard Time, Monday through Friday.

Ordering by fax:

Complete the order form or print the needed information on your own fax form. Fax your order to us at 318-948-6854.

Payment:

We accept Visa or Mastercard. Checks or money orders should be made payable to Creole Foods. For orders outside the U.S., we accept only Visa or Mastercard. Sorry, no CODs.

❏ Please send me _____ copies of **Tony Chachere's Second Helping** cookbook at $24.95 each (includes shipping and handling in the Continental United States).

Name _____

Address _____

City, State, Zip _____

❏ *Enclosed is my check (or money order) for $* _____
❏ *Please charge it to my*   ❏ *VISA*   ❏ *MasterCard*
in the amount of $ _____

Account # | | | | | | | | | | | | | | | | |

_____   _____
Expiration Date   Signature

❏ If you are purchasing a cookbook as a gift for someone other than yourself (or in addition to yourself), please check this box and write the name and address of the recipient(s) on a photocopy of this order form and mail it along with your form.